Finding Your Faith

DONALD DAVIS

WESTBOW
PRESS®
A DIVISION OF THOMAS NELSON
& ZONDERVAN

WestBow Press books may be ordered through booksellers or by contacting:

WestBow Press
A Division of Thomas Nelson & Zondervan
1663 Liberty Drive
Bloomington, IN 47403
www.westbowpress.com
844-714-3454

ISBN: 978-1-6642-4767-3 (sc)
ISBN: 978-1-6642-4766-6 (e)

Library of Congress Control Number: 2021921359

Print information available on the last page.

WestBow Press rev. date: 11/01/2021

Contents

Introduction

THANK you for buying this book. I believe that when you read this book and apply its principles, it will lead you to a better life. I am referring to a life of knowing and studying the Bible. Life is a roller coaster with its extreme ups and downs, creating fear inside a lot of us. I have come to know that it is not the ride that frightens us but the fear of not knowing what is coming next.

We ask the obvious questions: who, what, where, when, why, and how. Is this not the process we have followed our entire lives? Well, I want to show you a new way to a better life that will eliminate all your fears. I have learned the only way to eliminate your fears in life is to find your faith. Finding your faith will involve you building a relationship with Jesus Christ and knowing the core principles of Christianity.

It is my hope that while reading this book, you will turn to the Bible and begin a lifetime study that leads you to an eternal life with Jesus Christ. To start, you are going to need a rock-solid foundation upon which to live your life, identifying and organizing your priorities. Your foundation will consist of the five Fs: faith, family, friends, fitness, and finances. I have found the five Fs to be the best way to remember them.

First things first. You will come to know that your faith

comes first in everything you think about, everything you say, and everything you do. Throughout your daily activities, you will need to pray. So, not only will your faith come first, but you will also be faithful all the time. The system or process through which you live your life will become constantly, continually reliant upon your faith.

The least of your priorities should be your finances. In today's world, humankind's world view is based greatly upon instant gratification and focuses on the result rather than the process. But what good is it to be wealthy if you must lie, cheat, and steal to accumulate it? In our daily activities, we need to pray along the way. So not only does your faith come first; you should be faithful all the time. The system or process that you put in place to run your life must allow for constant and continual input from your faith.

Once you have your foundation in place, it is then time to establish your direction and work on your ABCs. When you began in school, the first thing you learned was your ABCs. Now that you are older and you are beginning your walk with Jesus, you will learn a different kind of ABCs:

Always
Believe in
Christ

When you give your life to Christ, it is not just for a moment; it is for eternity. Giving your life to Christ equates to accepting Christ as your Savior for the purpose of your spirit's eternal salvation with God in heaven and not with Satan in hell. When you give your life to the Lord, you will need the ABCs again. But this time I am recommending you find an …

Attentive pastor, a
Bible, and a
Church.

To develop your faith, you will need a closer relationship with Jesus. To do this, you will need to learn the Word of God by following direction from an attentive pastor, studying the Bible, and attending church on a regular basis.

Now that you have your direction for learning the Word of God, you need to filter everything you hear. Have you heard the phrase "a wolf in sheep's clothing"? There are a lot of misleading and dishonest wolves out there. It is critical for you to implement God's Word into your life. But in doing so, it is up to you to verify it is, in fact, God's Word. You will set up a process for sifting through the lies and finding the truth. When you read, watch, or even hear what you are being told is God's Word, you will put it through your process of investigation and interpretation before you can implement it into your life. This should be a process that is consistent in methodology. Remember, if something sounds too good to be true, it probably is not in the Bible.

With your process in place, you can filter out all the lies and take in just the truth. You may often hear Christians talk about "God's plan" and "core principles." Christians have come to accept that God's plan is the core principle of their belief. You will hear worldly scientists share theories and beliefs couched as truth that you will often come to know is their opinion of the truth. Various religions will add to the Bible or change the Bible to support their views. They could be acting as false prophets. When you read the Bible, you will learn what happens to false prophets.

When you give your life to the Lord, you are accepting and living the core principles of Christianity, and you will find yourself in a direct, personal relationship with Jesus Christ. When you accept Jesus Christ into your life, you become a humble messenger to share God's Word. And when you come to know that what you have learned about Jesus is real, you will want to share it with the world. But why will you want to share it with the world? Will it be because you feel special? Perhaps you think you have found something nobody else has? Or is it that you feel you are better than others?

The reason you follow the Lord is not for your glory but for His glory. Everything we say and everything we do should be about glorifying God. There is no place in heaven for the proud. When you are a Christian, you do not focus on wealth here on earth. Your riches are being stored for you in heaven. When you walk with the Lord, you have no fears. If you let anxiety take over your life, you will never experience the comfort of being in the arms of Jesus. People who turn away from God turn toward a life filled with fear.

We need God in our lives so that we can handle those moments we cannot handle on our own. We know that we need God to take care of us in those times where we are facing what we do not know. Knowing the Word of God prepares us for those difficult times in life where we do not have an answer for what troubles us. It is those times that we must fight our fears with faith.

Once you develop a righteous confidence in faith to fight your fears, you need to maintain it. Life's most difficult moments do not just happen once. Life will continually have its ups and downs. When you find your faith, it is not for just a moment. Maintaining faith requires a lifelong commitment. When you turn away from your sins and accept Jesus into your life, it is for eternity, and it is an undying devotion. That means exactly that. Life without Jesus in it is no life at all. The best way to have an undying devotion for Jesus is to stay focused on Him. We do this by studying the Bible, worshipping Him, giving Him praise, and by bringing others who may be lost to the Lord. Just imagine how great of a gift it is to lead someone to the Lord.

It has been said many times that the greatest gift of all is love. There are books written about love, songs written about love, and films produced from love stories. There are many who go their whole lives never knowing or feeling love. Many people do not even know how to love. Yet one thing is for certain—God so loved the world that He gave His only Son so that our sins could be forgiven. There is no greater love than the love God gives to you. When you leave this world and you leave a legacy of love behind, you have lived a life God wanted you to live.

Thank you for reading this book and for being open-minded. God gave us His only son, Jesus. Jesus was crucified so that our sins could be forgiven. You have been given free will to turn away from your sins and accept Jesus into your life. When you do so, then, and only then, will you have eternal life in the kingdom of heaven. It is my prayer that you come to know that God has a plan, and it is perfect. When you build a firm understanding of the core principles of Christianity, you will turn away from your sins and invite Jesus into your life. Then you can begin finding your faith.

Foundation—The 5 Fs

FOR more than thirty years, I owned and operated a concrete construction company. Among our many jobs was to form, place, and finish concrete foundations. Without a good foundation, no structure will last or hold up under stress. The same holds true in life. You need to have a strong understanding of the foundational five Fs: faith, family, friends, fitness, and finances. This is also the order of importance that the five Fs should be placed in your life, with your faith being number one on your list. The five Fs are nothing new. They have been around and have withstood the test of time. And believe it or not, there are different variations of them. Let us start with the 5 Fs that I know. Well, are you ready? Here we go.

Faith (my definition) is *a spiritual belief where proof is not needed.* Nonbelievers will argue to no end that there is no proof of that in which we believe. They love to hear themselves speak, and they base their facts on a place on the internet that cannot be found. If you're like me, you don't like to start arguments. But when you have a strong faith, you do not need to argue. You know what you believe, and no one can take that from you. My point is if you find yourself in an argument with someone about whether or not there is a God, do not argue with them. Turn away. You can't argue with the uninformed. I have found that their lack of knowledge comes from partially reading but mostly not studying the Bible. They will glean their truth from a newspaper, but they won't study the real truth in the Bible. Wish them well and walk away. I have learned in life that conversation involves one person who is talking to one person who is listening. Turns are then taken, and the listener will speak, and the talker will then listen. However, if someone speaks to a listener who refuses to listen, what is the point? Learning happens when you listen, not when you talk.

Faith is beautiful. It is one of the many gifts given to you by God. You can give it away and stop believing, but why would you do that? Is it because something bad happened in your life, and if there were a God, bad things would not happen to you? Let me answer that. It is because life is like a roller coaster; it has extreme ups and downs. One minute you are at the top, the next minute you are at the bottom. Good things and bad things are going to happen to all of us. That is just the way life is. But it is our faith in Jesus Christ and His promise of salvation that gets us through the tough times. If you believe in Jesus Christ with all your heart, mind, and soul, you will have the comfort of knowing you will have everlasting life. And remember, our God is a patient and loving God. I remind nonbelievers frequently that they have until their last breath to accept Christ, turn away from their sins, and still be given eternal life. But there is a catch-22. You do not want to wait until your last breath because you have no idea when your last breath will be. To put it in simple terms, that is one train you do not want to miss.

Faith is beautiful, but how strong should your faith be? It has been said that you should love the Lord with all your heart, mind, and soul. That sounds strong, but what exactly does that mean? Let us break it down and look at the heart first. The heart is literally at the center of your body. But figuratively, your heart is your creativity or imagination. Your heart is your hopes and your dreams.

I want to take a detour here for a moment and describe the differences I have observed on how men and women view the same thing. If you are a man and your wife is looking at a potential purchase and trying to decide whether or not to buy something, she will probably ask you, "How do you feel about this?" When my wife and I used to walk into the store to look for something, she would seek her own direction. She would grab a store clerk who was helping someone else, interrupt them, and ask where she might find that for which she was looking. I, on the other hand, quite typical of a know-it-all man, would seek my own direction and figure it out for myself. Further, I turned the search into a competition to see who would finish first. On many occasions, as I walked down the aisle preparing to claim victory, my wife would already be there waiting for me. You see, there are two different ways to arrive at the same destination. Returning to my original thought, women will use their heart or feelings to determine their direction.

If you ask a man how he feels about something, he will give you the strangest look, as if you are speaking a foreign language. The word *feelings* is seldom used in a man's vocabulary. If you are in possession of a valid man card, a different word will more than likely come out of your mouth. A man will ask the same question in a different way. "What do you think about that?" Now that sounds better. If I had used the word *feelings*, I could have had my man card ripped from my possession. Men rationalize. We use our minds, not our hearts. Now, at this point of the discussion, I am specifically saying that one way is not better than the other. And if you noticed earlier in the discussion, I said, "My wife would already be waiting there for me." But wait, you may say, doesn't there need to be a winner? Absolutely not. A trophy does not always get awarded. But in this case, everyone does get a trophy, and the trophy is your soul.

I have established both the heart and the mind with you. The third part of the equation is soul. When a man and a woman come together and give their lives to each other, it is one of life's beautiful experiences, second only to their personal relationship with Jesus Christ. When a woman (heart) and a man (mind) come together in a relationship, they will want to take their experience to the next level. Then they will add soul to their equation. Soul is how you express God in you. God is love. Love is the common thread that will bring your five Fs together.

Love is a popular word. I love my kids. I love to play eighteen holes of golf with my buddies. I love my wife. I love my God. Love, love, love, love. I have learned from our pastor that there are four types of love:

- storge—love my kids
- philia—love my golf buddies
- eros—love my wife
- agape—love my God

For God so loved the world that he gave his only begotten Son, that whoever believes in Him shall not perish but have everlasting life. (John 3:16 NKJV)

That is why love is so important in our lives. We want to receive love, and we want to give love. Love should be the common thread in all we say and all we do. That is why you want a personal relationship with Jesus Christ. You will find no love as great as the love Jesus gave by dying on the cross for us. Can you think of anyone else who let themselves be crucified in the way that Jesus did? I didn't think so. We and our loved ones around us need God's unconditional love in our lives. One of the main reasons I am writing this book is that it is my hope and prayer that you will find God's unconditional love and share it with your family.

Family (my definition) is *the foundation of our society that is established by God. Man and woman come together to procreate and raise their children with an understanding of Christian principles.* You are to love and honor your parents as well as your parents have loved and honored their parents. This is all part of the circle of life. The family unit is to include immediate family but also all extended family through either marriage, procreation, or adoption. Yes, this includes in-laws too. Ask your spouse's parents, "What is the difference between outlaws and in-laws?" Then tell them the answer: "Outlaws are wanted." Hopefully, they will find humor in this. If not, offer to do the dishes so you can buy time to think of something else to say. Sometimes humor is good, and sometimes it is not.

I never felt the need to defend myself with my in-laws. They welcomed me into their lives as if I were their son. They were always there in my life to lend a hand when needed, and they were always great to travel with. I always felt that my wife's parents were my parents. I was blessed. Nothing can ruin a marriage faster than when you are arguing about each other's parents. I believe that when you are married, you need to honor your in-laws as you would honor your own parents. This will go a long way in making your other half happy. You know what they say, "Happy wife, happy life."

There is so much information in the Bible that gives you guidance on families. If I were to include all the passages in the Bible that refer to families, you would be reading a book that was over a thousand pages. I will touch on the subject briefly. Honor your mother and father is one of the Ten Commandments. You do not have to always agree, but you do need to honor them for having brought you into this world and for raising you. God gave us the Ten Commandments, and we should live our lives and raise our families by these spiritual laws. I need to be careful here because I am talking about laws. But the fact is the Ten Commandments are the basis upon which the laws in our country were founded. There are those in this country who may say differently. They may say that the Constitution was based on principles found in the Magna Carta, not on biblical principles. And if you browse the internet, you just might believe them. But the truth of the matter is the Magna Carta was founded on Christian principles. Religion was a major influence on the Magna Carta because the church had power during that time. The church was a part of everyday life. The Magna Carta imposed legal limitations on the king of England's powers by creating committees that could overrule the will of the king. That is just one of many examples. If I get into telling you about the separation of church and state, this book might never end.

In our Constitution, we are given the right to freely worship what God we want to. Government has no authority over that decision. Do the research on your own and ask yourself one question. Why did the Pilgrims flee England and sail to America? Most sources will tell you that there were several reasons, but the main one was they were plain hardworking people who did not want to follow the Church of England, and they were able to settle in America. They had wanted to worship God in their own way. And that is where I agree.

I believe that nothing should come in between you and your personal relationship with Jesus Christ. Many religions have too many man-made rules and interpretations. The fewer times a story is told, the more accurate it is going to be. That is what leads me to tell you at this point the main purpose of me writing this book. After losing my wife to cancer, I prayed about a way that I could lead people to the Lord. I am not worthy of the task of teaching the Bible to others. There are many pastors who want to help you grow your relationship with Christ. And as this relationship grows, you will bring your family with you for the most important journey of a lifetime. It is my prayer that you and your family can develop the same faith over time that my wife had. God bless you with that thought, and now we will move on to friends.

Friends (my definition) *always have your back. A friend wants what is best for you, not necessarily what is best for them.* And that is where you need to make the distinction between who is a friend and who is an acquaintance. If you do not know, you really need to study the difference and know it. Again, a friend wants what is best for you. You may know people who say, "Hey, let's go get a drink." Is that what is best for you now, or are they just looking for someone to go get drunk with? If you have a problem and they are willing to let you bend their ear for an hour or two, maybe they are being a friend to you. They are if they are not interfering with you and your relationship with the four other Fs.

Obviously, a friend will not come in between you and your faith. If this person wants to start up a conversation about something that is contrary to what you believe, they are most likely in pain, and they want to feel better by bringing you down to their level. I am not referring to just physical pain. It could be mental anguish or even the death of someone close to them. There are many reasons they could be in pain. Always remember, a friend has your back and wants what is best for you. If your relationship is contrary to this, it is best to pay your check, tell them you will pray for them, and walk out the door. It is different if they are seeking help from you. When they are seeking help, they are not going to bring you down in the process.

When I think of this, it reminds me of my college days when I would lifeguard at a swimming pool during the summer. When you are trained as a lifeguard, you learn how to rescue people who are drowning. The golden rule is for you to save yourself first. You do not let the victim drown you. It does not do any good to have two casualties. The same holds true when you board an airplane. The flight attendant tells you to put the oxygen mask on yourself first, then on the one you are traveling with. You get the point.

It is not a bad idea to have friends at work. But remember that a friend will not ask you to do something against company policy or, worse, illegal. I was just having this conversation with my son who works for a large company. You never develop a friendship with a customer where you confide in them about something to gain their business that will benefit them and be against company policy. I have a good friend who did something like this, and when he got caught, his clients turned against him. When the IRS came knocking, these customers just wanted to protect themselves. And by doing this, they threw my friend under the bus.

My dad did not make much money, but he always said his satisfaction was in knowing that he could sleep at night because he had done nothing wrong to anyone. He was a good man. These are the same values I pass on to my kids. Weren't we talking about friends?

I have always believed that a true friend is someone who you could call at one in the morning if your car broke down, and they would come and give you a ride home. If you have friends like this, keep them for life. Friends like that do not come around often. I know my daughter has friends like that. She went to college in a big city. We never had to worry about her. She was surrounded by friends who would come to her aid at any time of the day or night. In her parents' absence, these friends were more than just friends and helped her unconditionally.

I remember when we had my wife's memorial service, my daughter's friends drove in from out of town to be at the service. They volunteered to serve the food and help clean up. When they told me of their intentions, I gave them a big hug, and I am not a hugger. My wife always assumed that role with everyone. I would see her hug strangers in airports. Maybe in some cases, all you need is just a good hug from someone to help you away from the edge of the cliff. A hug is a form of nonverbal communication that is just emphasizing to the huggee that everything is going to be all right. I could really use a hug right now, but this is a good time to talk about fitness.

Fitness (my definition) is *to be able to perform bodily tasks without pain; to be able to perform decision-making tasks without confusion; to be able to perform in a way spiritually that our God would approve.* I believe if we are fit, we can do the things we want to do in everyday life to our satisfaction. This definition is appropriate for your whole life. Let us dissect what I just said. I believe that to be fit, you must be more than just physically fit. If you look up fitness in the dictionary, they start talking about physical fitness. That is only part of what I am talking about. I am referring to a life without pain. When you are young, you do not focus on that. You focus on running, lifting, competing, and more. You confuse strength and speed with overall fitness. When you are young, you are lean, flexible, and quick to the task. But now that you're older, your body has broken down because you abused yourself at a young age.

Fitness also includes your immunity to sickness and disease. This one really hits home with me. I got diagnosed with Parkinson's disease when I was fifty-two. I immediately thought, *What did I do wrong?* Sometimes when it is your time, it is your time. When you get the news, you must pray about it and do the best you can. There are a lot of tough moments in life, but when the doctor tells you that you have an incurable disease that is going to get progressively worse, that is a big pill to swallow. You must treat your symptoms, pay attention to your areas of pain, address them, and hang on to hope that things can get better—a miracle, if you will.

Being physically fit is important, but just as important, if not more so, is to be mentally fit. I am very sympathetic toward people who suffer from mental illness. In today's world, people are put under a tremendous amount of stress. You keep putting yourself in a position where you are incapable of handling the pressure. There are many ways to deal with stress. When you get to a point where you see that you cannot accomplish what you set forth to achieve, stop. You are doing it to yourself. Stress is a result of not knowing the outcome of your effort. Be realistic in life, set reasonable goals, and be honest with those working with and around you. Do not ever set goals to impress others. You are setting yourself up for failure. In the end, it is not about what others think of you that matters. It is what you think of yourself that is important, and what God thinks about you is paramount. Be comfortable in your own skin.

I have talked about self-inflicted mental health issues, but what about genetic illnesses? Seek help, seek help, seek help! Again, I am very sympathetic with what you may be going through, but we live in a world that has a vast amount of information that is readily available with the use of a keyboard and mouse. Research your symptoms online, make a list of questions, document your symptoms, and get the appropriate professional medical help. The sooner you seek help before it gets out of control, the better off you are. You may not find your answer right away. You may take some wrong turns in your search. You may even get some bad advice. In my experience, I have attained more of a comfort level if I find someone who is going through the same thing that I am going through. Maybe they have some answers for you based on what they have tried and what works for them. That is why in some cases there are support groups for certain illnesses. But please realize I am no doctor. Seek professional help. It is your life we are talking about. And in most cases, you don't get a second chance or a do-over if you don't act now.

When you believe in God, the Holy Spirit is within you. Do you know where you are going after you leave this world? That is probably one of the most important questions you can ask yourself. Know where you are going and what you need to do to get there. Having the answers to these questions will take a lot of pressure off you and give you comfort. More than being temporarily happy, you are looking for a joy-filled life. What I call being fit spiritually is what is more commonly referred to as God's plan. God's plan is about salvation. When you mention salvation to a believer, right away they think of the John 3:16. This verse is the most important step you can take in your spiritual well-being. To fully know, accept, and apply this verse to yourself is what life is all about.

> For God so loved the world that he gave his only begotten Son, that whoever believes in Him shall not perish but have everlasting life. (John 3:16 NKJV)

When you accept this, you have taken a step that all Christians have taken. We would recite this passage in church almost every week—that there is only one God, and sin has separated us from God. But if we invite Jesus into our lives so that our sins can be forgiven, we will receive the gift of eternal life. Knowing where you are, where you are going, and how you are going to get there is really what you need to be focusing on. I am a Christian. I am going to heaven when I leave this world, and the way I am getting there is by believing that Jesus Christ is my Lord and Savior. By accepting Jesus and asking Him to forgive my sins, I will be given eternal life. That is what I call being spiritually fit. Now let's move on to the fifth F, which is your finances.

Finances (my definition) is *the acquisition and management of wealth to fund your lifestyle.* Do you live to work or do you work to live? And at the end of the day, just how much is really enough? I know it does not seem like a particularly good transition to go from spiritual fitness to finances. But when you find your faith, you will learn that God is in control of your life.

You must know and accept that you can worship only one God. Those who worship money will travel a foolish journey and then perish in the end. God will bless us with all we need to survive. It is extremely critical to understand the difference between earning money to buy things versus earning money to give us or others an opportunity to do things in our lives. Have you heard the old saying, "You can't take it with you"? Do you get remembered most for what you have purchased with your money or with the opportunity you were given because of what you have earned and how you have blessed others? It is better to give than to receive. And more importantly, we should give with our left hand, so our right hand does not know what we are giving.

If you have been blessed with good fortune, give something back. There is a story I would like to share with you. My wife and I were buying a house, and we called her cousin to do the home inspection. When I asked for the bill, he said, "It's on me, no charge."

"You can't do that. I'm paying you," I said.

He said, "Don, when I was starting out years ago in construction, you gave me a trailer. I'm doing well now, and I'm just returning the favor." I had honestly forgotten I had given him a trailer. In other words, the right hand didn't know what the left hand had given.

Often in life, it is not only what you give to someone but also when you give it to them. When people are starting off in business for themselves, they are usually operating on a shoestring budget, and they need all the help they can get. But when you give, do not stay around to be praised. If you want recognition, then you are not truly giving. A famous football coach once said, "When you achieve success or win, pass the credit." My favorite thing about watching a major sporting event is at the end when the victor says, "First of all, I would like to thank Jesus Christ. Without Him, none of this would be possible."

Right now, sit down and think about all the factors that need to be in perfect alignment for you to achieve financial success. Now, how many of these factors do you have direct control over? If you said under 10 percent, you are probably correct. But truthfully, it is probably more like less than 1 percent. And now that you have been blessed with wealth, do you realize how short-lived that is? Do you know how quickly, through no control of your own, it can be taken away from you? God provides us with everything we need.

A wise old salesman I worked with used to always say, "We spend a lifetime working so we can buy labor-saving devices." Really let that saying soak into your brain. It is true, and we do not realize it. How much is enough? Well, I recently read several books on Psalm 23. And I came to realize that when the Bible says, "He makes me lie down in green pastures," those green pastures are scarce sprigs of grass in a rocky field. God will not reward us with abundance because he does not want us to be distracted with a false sense of wealth and turn our attention away from Him. He is all we need to survive. I recommend that you study Psalm 23. One could spend a lifetime studying that passage. Don't just read it; study it and live it.

> The Lord is my shepherd;
> I shall not want.
> He makes me to lie down in green pastures;
> He leads me beside the still waters.
> He restores my soul;
> He leads me in the paths of righteousness
> For His name's sake.
> Yea, though I walk through the valley of the
> shadow of death,
> I will fear no evil;
> For You are with me;
> Your rod and Your staff, they comfort me.
> You prepare a table before me in the presence of
> my enemies;
> You anoint my head with oil;

My cup runs over.
Surely goodness and mercy shall follow me
All the days of my life;
And I will dwell in the house of the Lord
Forever. (Psalm 23)

Always Believe in Christ

I HAVE given you my five Fs and their definitions. It is my hope and prayer that this book can lead you to the Lord. Once there, that is as far as this book can take you. When you have accepted Christ, you need to …

> **A**lways
> **B**elieve in
> **C**hrist

For this, you will need another set of ABCs. You will need an …

> **A**ttentive pastor, a
> **B**ible, and a
> **C**hurch

An attentive pastor (my definition) is *one who leads a congregation by providing spiritual leadership; a pastor who is mindful and observant of others and is heedful of the comfort of others.* That basically means one who likes to see you listening rather than one who likes to hear themselves speak. I have listened to a lot of speakers in my life. A large percentage of them just speak. I would lose your attention rather quickly, and you would probably end up throwing this book away, if I focused on how much I know. This book was designed with the idea of how much you will learn. The title of this book is *Finding Your Faith.* I am staying within those boundaries of trying to convey to you how you can do that. Any more than that, and I would be crossing the line.

After you read this book, you will need to find an attentive pastor who is educated in the ways of teaching you the Bible. That is when the fun begins. When you begin your tutelage from an attentive pastor, you can hand this book off to someone you know who is looking for a better life too.

My wife and I were blessed to have a brilliant pastor who taught straight from the Bible. When a pastor is teaching, he needs to be careful not to misinterpret biblical passages. The pastor's teachings should be straight out of the Bible, and you should be studying the Word so that you are in a position, if need be, to question him if he gets off topic into nonbiblical principles or sayings. I emphasize that you want a personal relationship with Jesus Christ. If anyone comes between you and God, they are in your way. So, what are you waiting for? You now know the five Fs, and your foundation is in place. Now you can start the process of building your new life.

It is not where you have been. It is not even where you are. It is all about where you need to go. Who are you going to seek guidance from? When you are born again, you put all your faith and trust in Christ. You have accepted Jesus Christ as your personal Savior and that God has a plan for your life. If you have done this, you will be given eternal life in the kingdom of God. Let us briefly talk about religion because that is what your pastor represents.

When you search for a pastor, you need to know the direction in which he or she is traveling. You are going to believe in God, but which God? Everywhere you read, every religion has only one God. So which religion is real, and which god is God? If all these religions are monotheistic (believe there is only one God), which one is real? Which one is telling you the truth? It is not about all these religions. It is about the relationship between you and your God. Just remember, religions are in place to enhance your relationship with God. That is your direction. In the end, all of us will be judged by God. Know this: false prophets will be among those who will be judged the harshest for leading their fellow man down an erroneous path.

You need spiritual direction. Which religion do you choose? I chose my relationship with our Creator first, followed by a religious affiliation next, which supports my belief. This is a question we should pray about. God will give you answers when you ask in prayer.

Let us learn a little about monotheistic religions. If you do your research, you will learn that Christianity, Judaism, and Islam are all examples of religions that believe in one God. And which of these is the oldest? None of them. Many believe Hinduism to be the world's oldest religion, dating back more than four thousand years. But wait, creationists believe the world to be approximately six thousand years old. This might be a good topic to discuss with your new pastor.

We are talking about religions with one God. Is there a religion with no gods? There is. It is atheism. They have no belief in supernatural beings. If that is so, how were we created? I do not recommend atheism as a road one should travel. I would never ever close the book on our God. I would never want to be in the shoes of an atheist. I believe a large percentage of atheists are really agnostics. Agnostics neither believe one way or the other in a supernatural being. And I honestly believe a large percentage of them are waiting to jump off the fence onto one side or the other. They just want to be shown a fact first. I do not want to live a life based on facts all the time. There are going to be many times in your life when you do not have all the facts in front of you to decide. Then what? You need to put your faith in someone or something. I prefer to put my faith in Jesus Christ for all my decisions. Pray about it.

Probably the largest determining factor when choosing a religion is what religion were you raised on. Over time, as you grow older, like me, you may see things with a different perspective. You may want to know more and have a better understanding of what you believe. My wife and I wanted to have a better relationship with Jesus Christ, so we chose a pastor who taught straight out of the Bible. We believed that was the best way for us to raise our family.

I am not a judge. God is. I believe when choosing a belief system for you and your family, the strongest determining factor is the one that gives you the closest relationship with our creator. Another question might be, which belief do you and your family feel most comfortable with? There are a lot of questions to answer, and you need to take your time and get it right. You are talking about making a lifelong commitment, not just in this life but also in the next life. I have briefly talked about religions to give you a taste of how complex this subject can get. My intent is not to confuse you, but you need to understand that this chapter is going to deal with your direction in life.

Just to remind you, we laid the foundation with the five Fs in the first chapter, but now you need to head in the right direction. Let's have you learn a little vocabulary. The belief that God(s) exists is called *theism*. As you learned before, *monotheism* is the belief in only one God. When you believe in all religions, that is called *omnism*. And when you believe in the existence of a creator who does not have a relationship with you, you are a *deist*. Our founding fathers of our country were deists. I cannot imagine praying to a God that you do not have a relationship with. I need

Jesus in my life. It is my hope and prayer that you do too. God offers me hope. When you find the right attentive pastor, you will come to know that there is only one God, and He is very much a part of your life.

I have bounced around a bit on the topic of your pastor because they are an extremely important piece of the puzzle. They are responsible for your direction on how you study the Bible. By finding a pastor who is spiritually leading you in a direction that gives you a closer relationship with God, you have established an outlet where your pastor can also teach your family and friends. That is your hope—that your relationship will grow. After establishing a relationship with your pastor, your search for a Bible begins.

The Bible (my definition) is *a book containing the Old Testament and the New Testament and is considered the source of scripture.* The Bible is the textbook for Christians. Get a Bible that is comfortable for you to read. My wife had a Bible that had oversized print. It was easier on the eyes. Also, in my wife's Bible, where Jesus spoke, it was printed in red ink so you could distinguish between the human author's words and Jesus's divine words. And do not be afraid to write notes in your Bible so you can refer to them. Really important, have in your possession a Bible where you can easily follow the readings of your pastor on a regular basis.

Who wrote the Bible? The first five books of the Bible (the Torah) were written by Moses. After that, the authors were delivering the message of God by way of history, poetry, wisdom, prophecy, gospel, letters, and revelation. The Old Testament was written by common people, who were Aramaic, and by the upper class and government, who were Hebrew. The New Testament was written in Greek. The Bible has been translated into hundreds of different languages over the years.

Your pastor will be teaching out of the New King James Version (NKJV) or the New International Version (NIV) or something similar. Either version is fine. The first Bible I read was the Book (NLT) published by Tyndale. It was an easier read for someone like me. It was a thought-for-thought translation. Instead of being word-for-word translation from Hebrew and Greek, the ideas were expressed in a way ordinary people of our generation would relay them. William Tyndall was instrumental in the Hebrew and Greek translations of the Bible five hundred years ago. I still remember my favorite Bible verse when I first read the Book. It was out of the New Testament:

> What does it profit, my brethren, if someone says he has faith but does not have works? Can faith save him? If a brother or sister is naked and destitute of daily food, and one of you says to them, "Depart in peace, be warmed and filled," but you do not give them the things which are needed for the body, what does it profit? Thus also faith by itself, if it does not have works, is dead. (James 2:14–17 NKJV)

I could talk all day about what this Bible verse was saying and what it means to me. When I first read this verse, I was struggling with my outlook on life. And right there, I got my answer. What if tomorrow you opened the Bible and were reading—and suddenly your greatest question in life is answered. Now no two people are the same, and I am sure everyone has different questions they want answered. But one thing is for sure. The Bible is filled with a lot of answers. It is my belief that we should read the Bible, study the Bible, and live the Bible.

A few years ago, my wife and I took a trip to visit the Ark and the Creation Museum in northern Kentucky just south of Cincinnati, Ohio. That was quite the experience. You read in the Bible, and you try to envision what Noah's Ark must have looked like. Then in a moment, you are standing right in front of a life-size replica of it. And then you visit the Creation Museum and see all their exhibits with Bible verses on every wall of the building. To have read about this for years and then one day to see what your readings would look like in actual life-size depiction is overwhelming.

The one regret I have is my wife and I never visited Israel. You read about it every day, and then you think next year is the year. Well, I had decided 2020 was going to be the year, because not only were we going to visit the Holy Land, but we were going to see the *Passion Play* in Bavaria, Germany. This play performs every ten years. I had checked on the details. We found a church that was going. My wife passed away in March of that year. We never made the trip. There are no promises that you will be here tomorrow.

I mentioned we should read the Bible, study the Bible, and live the Bible. Reading the Bible can be done several ways. It can be every morning or every evening that you set aside time to read a few random passages from the Bible so you can stay focused on the Word of God. Your pastor could recommend a daily reading course where you read a few pages of the Old Testament and a few pages of the New Testament. Something like this takes about a year to complete the entire book. You could attend Bible study a once a week or twice a week and go over the reading then. Maybe you could take turns reading. The point is that you need to find some way to read the Word of God every day. You need to find some way to put the Bible in your hands at least once a day. It is like learning a language. If you do not use it, you will lose it. It is not enough to just read the Bible; you must make the effort to study it.

Studying the Bible may require more effort than you think. You can try to learn the content as you read, but there is more to it than that. What if you do not understand a passage and do not know what it means? What if you need more clarification as to the time and place of one of the books and what it meant during that time? What if you need a description of the time and place the author is trying to describe? All these are good questions that a weekly Bible study might be able to answer for you.

As I mentioned before, my wife taught a Bible study once a week, which was designed by a nationally known pastor. They had the resources to provide the coursework, the written materials, and the support. She really enjoyed that. When they last met, they had more than a hundred regular attendees. I never attended her woman's Bible study until she did her last one. I would do other things like help set up, or deliver materials for her, or even purchase items that were specially made for the group of women. One of my greatest moments in life was watching her deliver her last introduction at her last class. She was jaundice from her liver shutting down. She was weak from all the cancer treatments. She was tired of fighting the cancer. But, with the Holy Spirit in her, she delivered a perfect introduction for the attendees. What she could accomplish with the power of Jesus Christ was amazing. She knew she would be with Jesus in a few days, and that was what mattered the most to her.

We need to live the Bible every day. My wife lived the Bible every day. She would not take any shortcuts. She would never profit from something that was not right. And she put God first in everything she did. She was one who walked the walk. When it comes to knowing God, talk is cheap. God is everywhere, and He sees everything. If you are not living by His rules, you are not living the life He wants for you. With the power of God on her side, my wife could find her best moment on her worst day, because no matter what happened here on earth, she had eternal life waiting for her up in heaven. You can have that too. Now, what about the church?

Church (my definition) is *an organized body of believers worshipping God.* I believe it is not the building that defines the church; it is those who are inside collectively worshipping God with readings from the Bible, singing worship music, and coming together in prayer. Unfortunately, those who do not know put too much emphasis on the building rather than the body inside. Although I did see some examples in my life where the actual building did play an important role in worshipping.

A few years back, my wife and I were at a convention in Louisville, Kentucky. After we took a tour of a famous racetrack for horses, we drove downtown to get some lunch. As we were driving through some of the older neighborhoods, I kept noticing all the church steeples. It was quite a sight. From our vantage point, you would know where your church was if you were lost. Also, I noticed the beautiful architecture was aesthetically pleasing to look at. And most of these churches were rather old and still in operation, so it gave a testament to their longevity and stability. I guess if you are driving up to your church, or years ago walking up to your church, you felt good worshipping in a safe and comfortable environment.

When my wife was little, she always felt safe knowing she could look out the window of her bedroom at night and see the steeple of the church. Years later, she helped organize a Bible study that would gather at that church. She taught there for years. I guess you could say her life had come around full circle. Let me continue with the church.

An important thought is not just where you worship but who you sit next to when you worship. A lot of people want to sit together as a family and worship as a family. That is really a great way to honor your God, and there is absolutely nothing wrong with that. Unfortunately, there is just one thing I would like to bring up—the crying baby. When I was a kid going to church, you could always count on hearing a crying baby in church. If not one, maybe two or more. If I was focusing on those thoughts, obviously I was not paying attention to the service. In a nutshell, I was learning nothing. So why even be there if you are not getting anything out of it? For many years, my wife and I attended a church that took this into consideration.

When our kids were young, we would sit in a designated

cry room off to the side so we would not be a distraction at the service. You would have a more receptive environment for learning. Hence, that is why there is no loud talking in a library. And when our children became of age, they attended their own Sunday school while my wife and I sat in the main sanctuary. For someone like me who gets easily sidetracked, this setting was extremely conducive for learning. And when church ended, you could stop by the coffee shop on your way out, and I could make you a latte or a cappuccino. Our family worked in the church coffee shop on Sundays before and after service.

One more thought on who you are sitting next to in church. You can sit upfront so you feel more involved in the service, or you can sit in the very back so you do not feel like everyone is looking at you. I have a friend who sits in the very back so that the minute service ends, he is the first one in the parking lot, ready to go home. Be aware of those worshipping around you. This is a great opportunity to meet a new friend who shares the same spiritual belief. You could even meet several friends and start up a Bible study during the week. The point is get to know those around you because chances are you might be attending the same weekly service for many years.

Study the Bible, sing worship music, and come together in prayer. It is in your best interest that you select a church that teaches directly out of the Bible. You may want to take your Bible with you when you go to church, just as when you were in school, you would carry your textbook to class. Hopefully, you will know what passages your pastor is going to go over, and you can read them before the service starts so you will be better prepared. Unfortunately, that is not always the case, but it is okay if you have your Bible and you are following along.

I doubt this would ever happen, but in that rare instance that your pastor misquotes a passage from the Bible, you want to stand up in church so everyone can see you and point out his mistake. Not! If you want to keep your pastor accountable, address it with him in private later. If he takes offense or likes to misquote on a regular basis, it might be time to find another church, no matter how good the coffee is there. Fortunately, this rarely happens. Make sure you are in sync with your reading materials. Make sure the Bible you are using is the same translation that the pastor is using. Not all Bibles are the same, and you could get lost or frustrated. Ask the church if there is a recommended reading course of the Bible that you could be doing on your own. When I read the Bible cover to cover as I started my journey, that is what I did. And as support, the church may recommend books to read in addition to the Bible. I must be careful here because in the Bible, it explicitly states the following:

> And if anyone takes away from the words of the book of this prophecy, God shall take away from the Book of Life, from the holy city, and from the things which are written in this book. (Revelation 22:19)

That is why I wrote this book as a way of leading those who were lost to the Bible or to God. In my opinion, any writing concerning God after the Bible was written should be for the sole purpose of leading you to the Bible or for further understanding of the Bible—period!

One of my favorite experiences in church is to worship our God by singing. I would sing in the shower sometimes, I would sing in the car with my wife and kids on road trips, and I would always sing in church. I have always liked music, but I was never able to play a musical instrument. God did not bless me with that talent. I honestly believe it is a gift from God because every time I would try to play a musical instrument, everyone in the room would say, "God, please make him stop." When I would listen to music in high school, I was always driven by the beat of the music, and the lyrics, most of the time, were suspect. Most of the music I had listened to had absolutely no meaning. Not until my wife introduced me to the Christian radio stations did I finally get music with meaningful lyrics. When my wife took her last breaths here on earth, I lead our family in the singing of "I Can Only Imagine" by Mercy Me. It was a beautiful moment. Let us take a timeout from reading right now. Turn your computer on, and go to the internet. Look up the song "I Can Only Imagine." Get comfortable, play the song, and now worship our God by singing this song. Are you back with me? Can you imagine what you will do when you come face-to-face with our God?

Coming together in prayer is extremely powerful when led by a pastor in church. With your heads humbly bowed, you hold hands, and you collectively focus your thoughts and prayers up to God so He can acknowledge them. Some of my favorite memories are of watching my wife pray with our kids as she put them to bed. Many a night, she would pray together with them in our queen-size bed. Do you know why I call it a queen-size bed? Because when my wife and kids would fall asleep, they would take up all the space on the bed, and the "king" would have to sleep on the couch.

I have always enjoyed praying to God, although He rarely answers my prayers on the golf course. That is not important. But when a congregation comes together to collectively pray as one, that is awe inspiring. I have learned by listening to others pray in church that I will no longer pray for meaningless things like a good score in golf. I pray that those I love who are in pain will suffer no more. I pray for good health and for the safety of my children. I pray that someday I will be together again with my wife up in heaven.

As you have noticed by my writing, I have bounced around a little by mentioning the Bible in the church section. Or I may have elaborated on something else in another section. The reason for all this is that after you start your new life, you'll find that your attentive pastor, your Bible, and your church will all be working together as one. You will be listening to your pastor teaching, with your Bible open, while sitting in church. They all work together.

Let us take a break right now. Go back to the beginning of the book. Scroll down the list of chapters. Did you notice that if you take the first letter out of each chapter and put them together, it spells *faithful*? That is just a little test for you. As you are reading this book, are you the type of person who reads with an open mind and is receptive to positive change, or are you the type who has already made up their mind and is looking for one reason to slam the door on change?

It's the Process

I N chapter 1, you established your foundation with the five Fs. In chapter 2, you started in the right direction with the ABCs. So, what comes next? Well, as you start your journey to find your faith, what happens if you hit a stumbling block? What if you have a question and you cannot find the answer? You want to set up a process whereby you can go straight to the source and get the answer—not just any answer, the correct answer. *This is confusing, Don. What are you saying?* Everyone, at some point in their life, develops a process for finding out the truth. We are going to call your new process investigation, interpretation, and implementation. So, keep your I's(eyes) on where you are going.

Investigation (my definition) is *the process of systematic study, formal examination, or research.* It seems like when you do anything in this world, you have to follow a process. Whenever you take on a new project, you always start with the old *who, what, why, when, where, and how* process. You fill in the blanks and are ready to go. This is going to be a little different because we are talking about finding the truth. Let us start with this example. "How do I raise my children on Christian principles?" I do know that the focus of my search will be in the New Testament. The Old Testament tells us of the Jewish faith scripture, and the New Testament is the fulfillment of the prophecies from the Old Testament. Because the question is "How do I raise my children on Christian principles?" we could begin our investigation in the New Testament. In our walk with Christ, everything revolves around salvation. Children need to know God's plan for salvation.

> For God so loved the world that He gave His only begotten Son, that whoever believes in Him should not perish but have everlasting life. (John 3:16 NKJV)

And your children need to know this passage from the Bible:

> I can do all things through Christ who strengthens me. (Philippians 4:13 NKJV)

This verse gives your children encouragement. They will not quit the task set before them if they know they have Jesus to give them strength. Children need to know that they are not alone in this world. When the lights are turned off, God is still watching over them. Another passage I like is this one:

> Have I not commanded you? Be strong and of good courage; do not be afraid, nor be dismayed, for the Lord your God is with you wherever you go. (Joshua 1:9 NKJV)

This verse tells your children to be strong and that the Lord is watching over them.

As you become more familiar with the Bible, you will realize that it is the resource to find answers to life's most important questions. Passages, scripture, and doctrine can all be found in the Bible. You can ask your friends you sit with in church. You can bring it up at your weekly Bible study. You can ask your pastor. You can try a reliable source on the internet, but they all lead you back to the Bible. So, the more you study and the more knowledge you have of the Bible, that is your ultimate source for answering all your questions. I did mention the internet. You must be careful with the internet. The internet can be a good source or bad one. Remember there are those rewriting history to support their own nonbiblical beliefs. While researching on the internet, stay with sources you know that are recommended by your pastor and church. Steer clear of all the wolves in sheep's clothing.

Remember that while your children are young, they are extremely vulnerable. They can be influenced rather easily. It is widely known that all believers have the fear of God in them. I am not going to say that children should fear their parents, because that could cause other problems. They need to love, respect, and honor their parents. From the last chapter, they need to have a storge love for their parents. I have had many an argument over the years, telling people that parents should not try to be their child's best friend. Rather, they should try to be the best parents they can be. Parents often do a lot more for their children than their friends ever will. I remember taking our kids to the hospital on several occasions and being with them to the point where no friends would have made that kind of commitment. I believe that if your child thinks of you as a best friend, you are falling short of being a good parent. If my son were to tell someone, "My dad is my best friend," I would feel insulted. It would mean much more to me if my child said, "I have the best dad." My son is showing me respect by saying that. That is my opinion.

Respect is not given; it is earned. When you see children who do not respect their parents, that is a difficult environment to live in, and it is not conducive to teaching your children about the Bible. If they have no respect, their attention span is almost zero. If your children were taught the Bible, they would know the Ten Commandments. The one I am referring to right now is for your child to honor their father and mother. This is the first of God's Ten Commandments, to end with a promise that if you honor your father and mother, you will live a long life with many blessings.

Over the years, I have not seen eye to eye with my parents. My dad was a good provider for his family and never missed work. My mom wanted more out of life and therefore did not respect my dad. But not to be pulled into their trap of choosing sides, I just accepted them for who they are. I feel comfortable knowing I must honor my father and mother even with whatever shortcomings they may have. There are situations in life where you do not have to respect your parents, but I will not go into that right now. I believe if you are making the effort to read a book of this nature, you are trying to be a good parent. I went a little bit off course, but I feel it was an important topic to discuss with you.

We realize that the Bible is the primary resource for answers, and most every other resource plays a supportive role to the Bible. Just like I wrote earlier, this book was written with the intent to lead you to the Bible to find your faith. I believe all books of faith should be written with the intent of giving you a better understanding of the Bible. When you are in the process of investigating ways to answer your questions in life, remember what I just told you. There is no substitute for the book that was read by more people and has had more copies published than any other book in history. With that said, how can there still be people who do not believe the Bible? I cannot seem to figure that one out, just like I cannot figure out why some people do not like chocolate. It is what it is. With that said, we are moving on to talk about interpretation.

Interpretation (my definition) is *to either translate something or explain the meaning of it.* Now that we have found what we believe is the answer to our question, how do we interpret what we have found to determine what it means? With what I am discussing right now, we are somewhat doing both. When we pick up a Bible, we don't realize just how much effort went into the translation of the Bible from the original language it was written into the language we are now reading. How accurate of an answer we get out of the Bible is in part a direct result of how accurate of a translation was given. Are we trying to translate a Bible word for word when the version we are using is a New Living Translation version that translates into phrases? What would be the purpose of translating word for word? Maybe we might get the answers to our questions by following a general concept of the passage we are studying? To what extent do we need to dissect the Bible to properly interpret it? I would have to say that you need to know three key ingredients to this equation before asking any more questions: your audience, the translation, and the question.

First, you need to know who the audience is. Are you finding out this information for you, your family, or a Bible study? Is your audience going to be content with a basic answer, or do they need more detail? If you are finding your faith, I would have to believe that for now, a general concept of the Bible verse you are studying would suffice. You are trying to understand the various books, and you now want to know which books to go to for which questions. Remember there are sixty-six books in the Bible (in some religions, more). That is a lot of territory to cover. You may read the Bible once cover to cover. But that will not be enough. In my opinion, when you do more than just read, and you instead study the Bible, it is going to be a resource that you will go back to again and again for the rest of your life. In studying the Bible, you are going to know where to go to get your answer. For example, if you are looking for verses in the Bible that teach you wisdom, you may start with Proverbs. I mentioned before that I like the book of James—so much so that we named my son James. My dad's name is James. My oldest brother is named James, and he named his son James. As you can tell, I have all these reminders so I will never forget the name of my favorite book. But seriously, the book of James tells us about living a life of faith. It also tells us about faith without works. The point I am trying to make is you need to know the meaning of each of the books in the Bible so you know exactly where to go to when it's needed. Let us get back to your audience.

You want to get to a point in your study of the Bible where you can follow this process:

- Your audience asks you a question.
- You open your Bible and go straight to the book that gives you the information.
- You compare a few passages.
- You give your answer straight out of the Bible

You have just given an answer, and hopefully you have directly quoted one if not several Bible verses. God wants you to know His Word and where to find it. Know your audience. Know if they are friendly or hostile. Also know if they are well informed or uniformed and argumentative. When you know all this, you will know how to deliver your message. Your hope is that a message well delivered is a message well received. Let us talk a little about translation now.

If a message is well received, the proper translation was probably used. The Bible has been translated throughout the years from Hebrew, Aramaic, and Greek into hundreds of other languages throughout the world. And there are different manners in which they have been translated. For example, the King James Version (KJV) is probably one of the most accurate translations of the Bible. Billy Graham taught out of this version. The KJV was written in the 1600s in England. The KJV was then updated and given a more modern translation when the New King James Version (NKJV) was written in the 1900s.

You can appreciate the old saying, "It got lost in the translation." The fewer times it is written, the more accurate it is going to be. The only way we can make the process more accurate is to lessen the number of steps at the end of the process. Therefore, you need to have a better understanding of what you are reading so you can be accurate with your presentation. Let me give you an example of this process.

> Confess your trespasses to one another, and pray for one another, that you may be healed. The effective, fervent prayer of a righteous man avails much. (James 5:16 NKJV)

We know that the book of James teaches us about living a life with faith. What I get out of this passage is that God can heal us if we have complete faith in him. We need to confess our sins when we pray. When we live our life with Jesus Christ in it, our fears subside because of the strength He gives us knowing that He will bless us if we are right with Him. God loves us, and that is why He has given us His Word. It is up to us to read and know the Word if we are to be blessed by Him. Have you ever heard someone say, "I got really lucky"? When you walk with the Lord and you live a righteous life, God blesses you. You do not want to be lucky. You want to be blessed.

Do I feel blessed? I do not pray for a good score when I am golfing. I pray for the things in life that I have no control over. Translation: I have the free will to hit my golf ball the way I want to, and if it turns out the way I want, then fine. But do not waste your prayers on golf. Ask God to bless your day. Pray that the weather is good, that you are healthy, and that your family is safe. These are all things that you have no control over; only God does. I came across a saying years ago, and it stuck with me. It read, "Pray for what you want but work for what you need." If you are in tune with what I am telling you, you do not need my translation. Have faith in God, and He will erase all your worries and fears. Let us now transition into the question.

A question is a sentence that is worded such that it tests your knowledge by seeking information. Questions, questions, questions! Life is filled with so many questions and not enough answers. If you are of the select few, you may even have the answer before the question is asked. That is where we would all like to be. Sometimes life can be filled with twists and seem like one of my favorite game shows where you are given the answer and you must figure out the question. As confusing as this may seem, remember this: God has all the answers. If you are trying to find your faith, get as close to God as you possibly can. And for those who do not know God, where do they find their answers to life's questions?

The further I get into writing this book, the more frustrated I almost want to get because I just do not understand the logic of a nonbeliever. I have come to only one conclusion that they must see in their mind. If I were to look at life through their eyes, I would want the easiest path to take in life. Now I said the easiest, not necessarily the best or correct path. We need to know the difference.

Let me give you an example of a nonbeliever's rationale in life when faced with one of life's important questions. "Where will I go to college?" Ask yourself this question first, "Why am I going to college?" And you say, "To get an education." How noble of you, but is that the truth? You are racking up huge student loans to get an education? Face facts. I believe you are going to college to acquire the tools necessary to get a job that, if you did not have a college degree, you could not get. The truth does not hurt that much now, does it?

If we are going to college to have a career and not just a job, then why can't the schools just focus on a curriculum that pertains directly to that career? Why don't the companies that are hiring play a more direct role in determining the classes you need to take to get that degree and in turn get you that career-type job? Why are students forced to take so many classes that teach information that they might never use again as long as they live? Why can't we fill our elective class requirements with classes that we would find useful to us? The point I am trying to make is, why are state-funded universities teaching curriculums that benefit nonbelievers? Their argument might be, "If you want a Christian education, go to a Christian school." If that is the case, why do our property taxes pay for public schools and give minimal effort for schools of faith? I will end this argument before it gets going. You get the idea how the nonbeliever faction of society has set the standards and has manipulated the system so they can have the easy path.

If someone is spending a life sentence in prison, what is their focus in life? The answer is "How do I get out of prison?" The same logic is true with nonbelievers. Their focus in life is not to try to promote the best way of life for all people. They want to focus only on their immediate narrative. They want the easiest path because they do not want to do extra for anyone else. They may argue the same about believers, but that is not true. If you believe in Jesus Christ, the greatest gift He has given you is love. We are to love everyone, and we are to want what is best for everyone. To end this conversation, I will ask you this question: what do you want in life, the easy way or to love and be loved? You can see by the example given; we get the answers we are looking for by asking the right questions.

To get the correct interpretation, we need to know our audience, the translation, and the question. This is all part of the process. You will learn that in finding your faith, you cannot take shortcuts. There is no easy way. Sometimes you feel like giving up, and those are the times when you must dig deeper. At times, prayers feel like they go unanswered. But do they really? Sometimes we must look harder for the answer. Just remember this old saying, "life is not easy." We are now ready to finish out this chapter by discussing Implementation.

Implementation (my definition) is *the process of going through with a decision.* You may have the greatest ideas in the world, but if you cannot implement them, then they are just ideas. Good ideas don't pay the bills, nor do they put food on the table. You can get to a point where you know the Bible well, but if you do not live what you have just read, you have not found your faith. I want to give you an example of implementation by talking to you about sin. In reading the Bible, you will learn that we are sinful by nature. You will know on many occasions that we are not perfect. No one is perfect. The only one who ever walked this earth who was perfect had nail holes in His hands and died on the cross. But it is important for you to know that if you commit a sin, you can pray about it and ask God to forgive you. If you believe and are sincere in your prayer, God will forgive you. But what if you knowingly commit that sin again and again and again? Are you going to try to ask God for forgiveness? At this point, don't you think you are putting God to a foolish test. In the Old Testament, it reads:

> You shall not tempt the Lord your God as you tempted Him in Massah. (Deuteronomy 6:16 NKJV)

This was referencing what took place in Exodus where the people of Israel doubted that God was with them. In the New Testament, it says:

> Jesus said to him, "It is written again, 'You shall not tempt the Lord your God.'" (Matthew 4:7 NKJV)

And Jesus answered and said to him, "It has been said, 'you shall not tempt the Lord your God.'" (Luke 4:12 NKJV)

It is written in the Bible, and it is clear what God expects of us. We have investigated the subject of sin. We have interpreted what God expects of us concerning sin. We found it in not only one place in the Bible but in three places. Now, with all this on our hands, God expects us to implement in our lives what has been written for us. It can't be any clearer than that.

To go one step further, we must ask ourselves, "Did I knowingly or unknowingly sin?" We go back to the Bible:

For if we sin willfully after we have received the knowledge of the truth, there no longer remains a sacrifice for sins, but a certain fearful expectation of judgement, and fiery indignation which will devour the adversaries. (Hebrews 10:26 NKJV)

And if I read through the book of James, it says:

Therefore, to him who knows to do good and does not do it, to him it is sin. (James 4:17 NKJV)

Here is a verse out of the book of James. It encourages me to be faithful. I am not telling you to go out and read the book of James right this minute. There may be other books in the Bible that can have that same effect on you. There are sixty-six books (or more) to study, so after you get to know them, you may find that special meaning in one or two of them. No two authors write the same. They may witness the same thing happening, and they will find two different ways to write about it. Every author has their own style of writing.

If you have read this book up to this point, you have come

a long way. Let us recap a little. You have your foundation. You learned the ABCs, and you have your direction. You have your eyes, or I's (investigation, interpretation, implementation), focused now on finding the truth. If you have stayed with me thus far, I have faith in you that you are ready for the truth. Before we go there, let us pray about it.

"Lord, I pray that You give me wisdom to make the right choices for my family and myself. You are an awesome God, and it is my desire to want to know You. Lord, I have been lost for so long, but now I have found You. Lord, I pray that You bless this journey that I am on to find my faith. Lord, my life is empty without You in it. Lord, You are patient, and I know that this journey will take the rest of my life. And, Lord, I know You love us because You died on the cross for us. Lord, when I take my last breath, I want to have eternal life with You up in heaven. In Jesus's name, I pray. Amen!"

Now relax for a minute. Find a relaxing Christian song on the internet, play it, and close your eyes. Worship, praise, and give thanks to our God ...

When you are ready, we will go on to the next chapter. God bless you ...

The Truth

Then you shall know the truth, and the truth shall
make you free.
—John 8:32 (NKJV)

THE truth (my definition) is *being in sync with fact; beliefs
that are reality; the opposite of lies, falsehoods, and unproven
statements.* If you are a Christian and you are studying the Bible,
you are searching for the truth. If you are a scientist and you are
conducting experiments, you are searching for the truth. Are
you searching for biblical truth or scientific truth? What is the
difference? Let us look at the two truths. After you finish reading
this chapter, you will begin to know that the Bible is the absolute
truth.

To determine what you are going to believe for the rest of
your life and your spiritual life beyond this life to be the absolute
truth, you must do the research for yourself. I do not want you
just to accept what I am telling you. I want you to study the Bible
and come to an understanding for yourself. My main purpose for

writing this book is to help you to find your faith. The only way you are going to find your faith is with the following:

A personal relationship with Jesus Christ our Savior.
By reading and studying the Bible to know the Word of God.
Church involvement and worshipping with other believers.

As you can see, reading this book is a start in the right direction. The Word in the Old Testament has been written for thousands of years. The Word in the New Testament has been written for over 1,500 years. Don't you think that if it were not the truth, scientists would have disproven it by now? You would think that as intelligent and as educated as they are, they could have conducted their own research and come up with a solid argument to prove their point. The best hypothesis they can come up with is evolution or the big bang theory. I am almost embarrassed to call them scientists. Unfortunately for the scientific community, they are led by extremely big egos. I believe many scientists are self-centered, and they want to focus on just what it takes to prove their theories. They are not open to the realm of investigating other different theories when their work is being scrutinized. When a scientist has their work proven wrong, they lose their status in their respective field. They also lose potential grant money from either the government, large corporations, or wealthy donors.

Fortunately, there are scientists who are not driven by recognition. These scientists put in endless hours working on research to find cures for various diseases, solutions to problems, better ways to grow and harvest foods, and the list goes on. These scientists have earned my respect because they are devoting their time and effort to helping humankind. When certain scientists are devoting their time and effort to try to disprove the Bible, just how are they helping humankind? They pour all their energy into fabricating falsehoods to slander a belief that centers around love. If they do not appreciate a large part of society that promotes love, they must be siding with the opposite, hate. From what I have witnessed in life, it is awfully hard to show love to those who have spent a lot of effort hating you. Because Christianity centers around love, it is often necessary to keep your friends close and your enemies closer. Nothing angers a nonbeliever more than to have a Christian show love and support toward them while they are spending all their effort in hating what you believe.

I am touching on a subject that is close and personal to me. I said earlier in this book that I lost my wife and best friend of thirty years to cancer. In addition to that, I have Parkinson's disease. The list goes on and on. I am not going to waste my time and your time detailing all the bad things that have happened to me in my life. I would rather spend that effort trying to understand why someone would want to reject our God and turn away from Him. In this case, I would like to change the future rather than dwell on the past. I believe that we need to understand the past so we can get answers to these questions that are focused on disbelief. There are two people who are close to me that I love very much. I want to share their stories with you as examples of the message I am trying to relate to you.

The first person lost his wife to cancer. Growing up, he was the most intelligent person I knew. He was brilliant. It amazed me how he could create and invent. I would look to see what he made with his two hands every day. When you saw the fruits of his hard work, your jaw would just drop. When I was young, he moved away. He was always a motivated, hard worker. He was self-sufficient and did not ask anybody for anything. He had earned my respect. Then one day, the bad news hit home. His wife had cancer. We were all stunned. Only now after my wife has passed can I understand what it is like to lose the love of your life and to not be able to live the rest of your life with someone you had built your world around. Unfortunately for people like myself who have lost their spouses, life goes on. You must get going every day and do what you need to do to survive. You cannot give up. You cannot quit. I discovered something that he never did. I realized that no matter what happens to me or whatever is taken from me, no matter how bad it gets, Jesus Christ is there for me.

Life is like a roller coaster; you have your ups and downs. No matter how scary things might seem, you must hold on tight to what you know. You must have faith that God is there with you. I get it. It is unfair sometimes what happens in life, but we cannot dwell on the past. You must focus on today and tomorrow. It does not matter to God where you have been and what has happened to you. What matters to God is that you invite Jesus Christ into your life, you turn away from your sins, and you have eternal life in the kingdom of heaven. Someday, I will see my wife again up in heaven. That is the hope I am hanging onto. The love story is not over yet.

The other story I wanted to share with you again involves cancer. This person has always been there for me through thick and thin. I have always looked up to him. And today, I still do. I did things in my life when I was young and stupid that I am not proud of. And one time, years ago, I did something that caused him hardship, and I never had the guts to look him in the eye and apologize to him and let him know how sorry I was for what I had done. They say that time heals all wounds. Well, that wound still, to this day, festers inside of me because I did not handle it the way I should have at the time. Again, I was young and stupid at the time. As time passed, he forgave me, but I still have not forgiven myself. He is a man I would do anything for. He has been with me and has checked on me almost daily since the passing of my wife—if just to talk on the phone with, to share a sandwich with, or whatever. This man who I have always looked up to has been there for me during the most difficult time of my life. He is probably the most honest person I know. He has never been driven by money, and he is all about doing what is right. I could go on all day about his positive traits.

Now that I have tooted his horn, there is only one thing in his life that I question. He has not accepted Christ. If there was one person in this world that I believe lives by Christian principles, it is him. It has always been a touchy subject. A few years ago, he went to the doctor to have some cancer taken out. It was a small procedure, and he was in and out in one day. Time passed, and one day he shared his story with me. I listened intently to every detail, and then he turned down a path I never would have taken. He said something that I have heard from many nonbelievers in the past. "If there were a God, how could I get cancer?" I have told this story to no one until now. At this time, I would like to share these Bible verses with you:

> Jesus said to him, "I am the way, the truth, and the life. No one comes to the Father except through Me." (John 14:6 NKJV)

> My brethren, count it all joy when you fall into various trials, knowing that the testing of your faith produces patience. But let patience have its perfect work, that you may be perfect and complete, lacking nothing.
> (James 1:2–4 NKJV)

I know what you are thinking right now. With so many books in the Bible, why am I quoting James so often? As I said before, the book of James deals with faith. And the title of this book is *Finding Your Faith*.

So, why do we get cancer? Why do we suffer? Is God being unfair? Nonbelievers do not know why we get cancer. And nonbelievers do not know what good can come out of something so painful and with so much suffering. But each situation is uniquely different. God loves us and wants to be in our lives. Pain and suffering are inside of us for a reason. God wants us to walk in faith and be submissive to him. When bad things happen in our world, it is so we can be drawn closer to Him. Even though it may not seem like it, He loves you and wants you to stay close to Him. Quite often, bad things happen to us to get us ready for something of more consequence in the future. By doing this, He is trying to lead you to have a closer walk with Him. You cannot possibly know what is fair and unfair with God. You do not see the circumstances that will occur in the future. But if you follow on His path, you can avoid trials and tribulations of a greater magnitude.

This would be a good time to test you and see what you would do. Let us say you are in a store and a young man walks in pointing a gun at the store clerk. The clerk presses the alarm that notifies the police. The gunman then shoots the clerk. As the gunman goes to open the cash register, a police sergeant comes through the door with his shotgun drawn toward the gunman. You are now in the line of fire. Your only option is to either get behind the police sergeant or the young gunman. What would you do? I would have to say that a great majority of people would get behind the police sergeant. That would be the wise decision.

Let us take that test again, but let us make two changes. Let us eliminate the young gunman and substitute Satan in his place. And let us do away with the police sergeant and put God in his place. Now which one do you get behind? I know you would make the right decision and say God. But the question I have is, who are the ones who would answer Satan? As easy of a test as this is, there is still a percentage of people in this world who would side with Satan no matter how obvious the right decision in life is. Those are the lost souls who need to find God. Those might be the nonbelievers who have so much hate and resentment built up inside of them they just will not trust God.

The Old Testament was proven with the discovery of the Dead Sea scrolls. The New Testament was proven because of the eyewitness testimony about the prophecy that was fulfilled. No matter what proof you present, there will be a percentage of the population who will not accept that there is a God. With some nonbelievers, they are so self-centered, like those certain scientists are, that they have gone down the wrong road for so long that they feel it is too late to turn around and walk it back. It is a pride issue of being wrong. And what does the Bible say about pride?

> Pride goes before destruction,
> And a haughty spirit before a fall.
> Better to be of humble spirit with the lowly,
> Than to divide the spoil with the proud.
> He who heeds the word wisely will find good,
> And whoever trusts in the Lord, happy is he.
> (Proverbs 16:18–20 NKJV)

I am being led right now to go a little off course of what I intended. I just want to share what just happened to me, and I hope in some way you can benefit from it. I did not sleep well last night. I was up every hour of the night, walking around the house and going to the refrigerator to drink some cold milk. At about six o'clock this morning, I rolled over in bed and grabbed my phone off the charger on the nightstand, like I do every morning. I scrolled through the phone to see if there was any critical national news that I needed to make myself aware of before I started my day. I briefly ran down the headlines and saw nothing I needed to know about right then. I was going to switch over to read my verse of the day and then go hop in the shower because I had to be somewhere. I had to go and get ready.

As I was getting ready to put on the verse of the day, the screen suddenly changed on its own. *What just happened? Okay, I will just click my smartphone and change the screen.* I touched the screen, and it went blank, kicked back on, and put me back on this same page that I didn't request. *What is so important about this screen that You want me to see?* I looked, and I saw a story about a famous Hollywood actor. I have seen a couple of his movies. I enjoyed watching him. With the movies I have seen him in, he always came off as a tough guy who could probably handle his own. But for some reason, I thought when he is closeup to the camera, his face seems to be telling a true story. To me, he is very believable in his roles. Then I thought, *Okay, I will read about him.* I was shocked after the first paragraph. He was the youngest of nine kids, his mom and dad got divorced, and he spent time in prison. Wow, I did not know that. I wiped my eyes so I could focus a little better and continued to read on. *I have thirty minutes to finish, and I must leave the house. I will continue.*

I wanted to know about his time in prison and how he turned his life around. That was all I cared to find out right then. I quickly read over the article and found it. I wanted to make sure of what I found. I clicked on my search engine to find out how he turned his life around. Another story came up, so I clicked on it. As I read on, the story gave me what I was hoping to find. When he was in prison, it was a priest who never gave up on him that helped him turn his life around. The story did not give any details, but I got what I wanted to read. The story went on to tell that he starts every day praying, and he ends every day in prayer. From prison to prayer, wow. He is now my favorite actor. Well, let me slow it down a little. I do not really endorse anything Hollywood does. I even went as far as to turn off my cable television. Yes, I am one of those who has pulled the plug. But if a story is true, has Christian principles, and is inspirational, I have got to share it. Now that is how I started my day. Oh, this is my Bible verse for today:

"Most assuredly, I say to you, he who hears
My word and believes in Him who sent Me

has everlasting life, and shall not come into
judgement, but has passed from death into life."
(John 5:24 NKJV)

I am going to let you think about that verse. It might be a
good time to search the internet and see if you can find out more
about this actor turning his life around and what the priest might
have said to him. But more importantly, I am focusing on you.
Take some time for yourself. Put on a Christian song or turn on
the radio to the Christian music station. (Once you have it on
Christian music, take the channel knob off the radio and hide it.)
And now, praise God. Give thanks for today. Let us pray:

"Lord, thank You for this wonderful day. Thank You for all
Your blessings. Thank You for the way You work in my life. I
now know that we are all sinful by nature. But I also know that
the closer I get to You, my sins will be forgiven. Lord, it is my
desire to have a relationship with You not just today but every
day. I pray in Your name, Lord. Amen!"

I want to take some time and reflect on what happened this
morning. Was it coincidence or was God talking to me? Why did
I want to share that with you? I believe that because it was the
truth. This chapter is focusing on the truth. I believe that if I can
find anything out there or even if it comes to me unannounced,
and it is a story that can help to bring you to the Lord or lead you
into having a closer relationship, you are going to hear the truth.

Let us continue. I believe God wanted me to share that with
you because there are a few things in this world that can turn your
life around and lead you to the Lord. True inspirational stories
just happen to be one of the best ways for you to turn to the Lord.
At this point, I would be successful in my mission if you handed
this book to a nonbeliever, picked up the Bible, and started your
journey of reading the greatest book ever written. Otherwise, let
us continue. I will now pray for direction on how to help you
find the Lord and lead you to the Bible. I am praying that God

gives me the words. I pray that He uses me to deliver his message. You see, I am not worthy. I am simple, broken, and hanging on to life. But I am holding on to the Lord's ledge.

The Lord's ledge is where I am at tonight. This is going to sound more like a journal than a book, but here we go. After I finished writing, I took an old friend out to lunch today. We met at my aunt and uncle's restaurant downtown. My family has a long history of being in Tucson, Arizona. My family goes back generations of living here. I have family that years ago built some of the original churches in the historic area of downtown Tucson. My aunt and uncle own and operate the oldest family-owned Mexican restaurant in the United States. My aunt has written many cookbooks, of which I have copies. When I have some spare time, I open one of her cookbooks and make something. I could go on for a few chapters about their restaurants, but I need to stay on track here.

When I met my old friend for lunch, we sat at the table, and our conversation picked up where it left off almost forty years ago. We played baseball together years ago. We began the conversation with the usual old stories. I like to tell people that I was going to play professional baseball, but one little thing kept me out of the big leagues. After I have gotten their full attention, I tell them the truth: lack of talent. I wasn't any good. That is why I did not make it. Everybody likes that one. It always breaks the ice. But it is the truth. Some people like to bend the truth to fit their narrative. Some people like to tell half-truths. Some people like to flat-out lie. I like to tell the truth till it hurts.

When we got done with the usual meaningless, typical sports-related guy talk, we talked about our kids and family. I was so excited to tell him I was writing a book. When our conversation started to focus on faith, I was so excited to talk about my faith. We talked about the religions we were raised in. I told him why I had turned my attention to studying the Bible and that I was working on writing a book. We had ripped up our man cards and were talking faith. But more importantly, we were telling the truth and talking about the truth. What an exciting and productive conversation we had.

I believe in today's world, we waste a lot of time trying to be funny, telling stories and making conversation about things that don't matter in life. Why? Because it is simple and easy. What I realized today is I get excited about telling people what I am doing. I am writing a book. It is a book that I hope will lead those who are lost to the Lord. In this book, I am telling the truth. Many people who are lost have been lied to for too long. Well, it is time to turn in. I received a call tonight, and I rushed over to my father-in-law's house. My father-in-law passed away.

It is the next morning, and I did not sleep well again last night. I am going to pick up where I left off last night. When I got the call from my wife's uncle, I rushed over to my in-law's house. When I got there, I noticed the back door was locked. That is the door I always went through to enter their house. So, I walked around and went in through the front door. Then, like a ton of bricks landing on me, it hit me right away. The last time I had been through the front door was three years ago when I was helping the driver from the mortuary carry my mother-in-law's body out the front door and into the hearse.

So, here we are three years later, and now my father-in-law will be with his wife for eternity. All the memories that were made in that house. There is one thing I can take away from what happened last night that I would like to share with you. You have a choice in this world when you make money. You can either buy stuff or make memories. My in-laws were all about making memories. I am sorry for being so blunt, but that is what it really boils down to—stuff or memories. I will take memories. My father-in-law would not give you a dollar out of his wallet. But if you needed help with something, he would break his back to give you a hand. He was that way. Stuff did not matter to him. Why do some people accumulate all this stuff their whole life when they know that they cannot take it with them? There is not that much room in an urn or a coffin. My in-laws gave me a gift by showing me how they travel. We went on a lot of trips together over the years. I learned from them some valuable concepts for traveling. It is not what you buy; it is who you meet. It is not about money spent. It is all about who you spend time with. And of course, comfort outweighs excitement.

I talked quite a bit with my wife's cousin last night. He was saddened by his uncle's passing. He wanted to know if his uncle knew the Lord. He was concerned about his dad and how he was handling the loss of his brother. At times like these, I have learned over the years that there is nothing you can say to make it any better. Some people try hard to come up with the perfect saying, but it always comes up short. I believe that God has given us two ears and one mouth for a reason—so we can listen twice as much as we speak. It is difficult to learn anything when you are busy talking and not listening. At times like this, you need to be a good listener. My wife's cousin is just that, a godly man and a great listener. When my wife passed, he came alongside of me spiritually and spoke God's words to me. And at the right time, he was a good listener.

I will give you a good analogy. I have fixed a lot of broken water pipes in my life, and sometimes you must let the water run out of the area of pipe you are fixing before you can cut the pipe and make the fix. If you do not let all the water run out, you might still have a leak after the repair. I believe that is the approach a good Christian counselor will take with you at a time like this. They will be a good listener and let you get it all out. And when the time is right, when it is your time to listen, they will jump in and make the repair.

After several phone calls with a concerned Christian cousin, the shoe was on the other foot, and I was going to lend a hand to their family. So, at this moment, I must get the guest room ready for my wife's uncle, who will need to stay here in town a couple days out of the week. He is quite the story himself. He is eighty-two and is still working as a doctor. He comes into town to work at the clinic a couple days of the week. I am looking forward to helping him after all he has done for me and my family throughout the years. He was staying with his brother, but all he will have now is memories of time spent with him. I believe at times like these, it is best to keep the memories and focus on the present and the future. Do not dwell on the past. You cannot change it. That holds true with a lot of things in life. I know he has a good grasp of what to do, and he will be all right.

The truth hurts. Have you heard that saying before? We are going to make a change in direction so I can finish this chapter for you. I also like this saying: it's better to get hurt by the truth than to be sheltered in a lie. I guess the best definition of the truth is it is the opposite of a lie. And the best definition of a lie is it is the opposite of the truth. When the Word of God is read in church, we respond by saying, "Amen" (the truth). So that must mean that anything that is spoken contrary to the Word of God is a lie. It is all black and white. There are no gray areas. You either believe in God or you do not. Life is not about doing what is easy; it is about doing what is right by our God. Period!

Let me finish this chapter with what you really need to know. The truth is that the only way to get to heaven is through Jesus Christ. You can waste away in the world, or you can live an eternal life by turning away from your sins and inviting Jesus into your life. I just lost my father-in-law yesterday, so I want you to pray with me right now.

"Lord, I want to lift my father-in-law, Walt, up to you. He was a good man, Lord, and I pray that he found You before his last breath. Lord, we know that to have eternal life, we need to turn away from our sins, and we must invite You into our lives before we take our last breath. I do not know why we watch the world when we need to look to You Lord for salvation. Lord, we ask for Your comforting love at this time to soften the loss, and we believe that he is in a better place with those loved ones he had lost before him. Thank You, Lord. We worship You, and we give You praise. In your name, we pray. Amen."

I used the word *comfort* a couple of times, and I am going to end this chapter praying that you find comfort in your life. Our God loves us, and He wants us to love Him. There is no greater feeling in this world than to know that God is there to comfort us when we need Him. He wants so much for us. We need so much from Him. He wants more than happiness for you. He wants you to have a life filled with joy. Happiness in this world is so temporary, but a life with God in it is joyful. True joy with God in your life is what I pray for you. May God bless you in your journey to find the absolute truth.

Humility

I MENTIONED in the last chapter we are given two ears and one mouth. This chapter is going to expand on that saying. I believe that God gave us two eyes, two ears, and one mouth for a reason. It is so that we will look at what is before us. We will listen to the needs of others. We will learn how to apply God's Word in our lives and in the lives of those around us. There are so many ways you can interpret what I have just laid out to you. You can even say we are given two arms to help others and two legs to walk toward those in need. But the most important thing we need to focus on is when we learn the Word of God, we are to humble ourselves. We are to be neither arrogant nor boastful. We are to be what God wants us to be—humble.

Humility (my definition) is *a modest opinion of oneself, to be humble*. Humility is hard for some and easy for others. We are sinful by nature. It is written twenty-seven times in the Bible, detailing how we are sinful by nature. Pride is sinful, and on the other end of the spectrum is humility. When you win a race, win a contest, or get first in anything, pass the credit. Be humble. I know it is hard to do. Your first instinct is to bask in the glory. But remember, nobody wants to listen to somebody tell them how great they are. Everyone wants to listen to you tell them who you followed for how to get there.

Have you ever noticed that when you tell someone you lose a lot of weight, where you went, and how you did it, they ask you a ton of questions? They are not asking these questions to listen to how great you are. They want to know where and how because they want that for themselves. And that is the best time to help change someone's life. Right at that moment. Take that time to give all the glory to God. There is no better time to praise the Lord than when you are on top and everyone is watching and listening. And when you pass the credit, if you are giving the credit to your God, make sure to start off by saying, "First of all ..." Jesus Christ always gets top billing because without Him, none of this would be possible.

Wow, you have won the race, and you have just passed the credit. You have come a long way. Let us think of other reasons to pass the credit. When you talk yourself up, you don't realize what you are doing to yourself. You are raising people's expectations of you. You have heard the old saying, "You're doing it to yourself." You are letting your pride take over. What does the Bible say about sin—oops, I mean pride? There are more than one hundred verses in the Bible that address pride. How about if we go to the book of James. Familiar with that book yet? I thought you might jump ahead of me and read the book of James. Let us try this:

> But he gives more grace. Therefore, he says:
> "God resists the proud,
> But gives grace to the humble." (James 4:6 NKJV)

> Do you see a man wise in his own eyes?
> There is more hope for a fool than for him.
> (Proverbs 26:12 NKJV)

Just like the book of James focuses on faith, Proverbs teaches us wisdom, humility, fear of God, and much more. King Solomon wrote the book of Proverbs. If I need words of wisdom, I go straight to the book of Proverbs.

Knowing what to look for and where to find it are keys to reading and studying the Bible. I wish more people would say, "I am studying the Bible," rather than "I read the Bible." I think in a lot of cases, when somebody says, "I read the Bible," they follow it up with their personal judgment of the Bible.

First, they have an opinion about the Bible. And second, who cares to hear their opinion of the greatest book of all time? And hey, that is a sin. It is God's job to judge. As you can see, you can get yourself into a lot of trouble and quickly when you do not check your pride at the door. When someone says, "I am studying the Bible," it shows that they are making the effort to know God because they are focusing on the present and the future. That is what God wants us to do.

To look (my definition) is *to focus on a specific direction*. Let me just interrupt this thought for a minute. I was starting to stumble a little. I was hesitating on a way to start this chapter. I sat back in silent prayer, and then my verse of the day came across the screen of my computer. It read:

> Your word is a lamp to my feet and a light to my
> path. (Psalms 119:105 NKJV)

Like the book of Proverbs, the book of Psalms is an excellent source to seek wisdom. There are 150 psalms, with David having written about half of them. The book of Psalms contains sacred song or hymns, poetic in nature, dedicated to God. I believe this verse of the day came right at the perfect time. There are so many ways I can go with this. My mind is racing right now. Let me try this: life is seen with more clarity when you look at it with humility in your heart. There is a good reason why when you go to a show, they never seat the spectators on the stage. If you are going to have God in your life, you need to take a distant back seat to him. You need to put on your humble hat and put your pride aside. Being prideful clouds your vision. Wow, I got so excited mentioning Psalms that I went all poetic on you.

How do we look at life? That is a great question to start with. You are given a choice in life. Would you rather look down on people or look up to God? Like I said earlier about my definition of the word *look*, we need to focus on our direction. We need to look to God—period. We need to look to God for all our needs. God will provide us with all we need to survive. Our vision gets a little cloudy when we think of how we are going to look at life. Ask yourself this: do you want to be fat and happy, or do you want to be lean and joyful, living a life with the Lord in it?

I was watching a comedian on the internet, and he seemed straightforward and funny. Unfortunately, humor distracts us in life and sometimes in a negative way. We must be careful choosing who we listen to. I laughed at this comedian's jokes and thought, *I am going to show this to my son.* This comedian was from the South, and he weighed over four hundred pounds. Fat and happy, right? Wrong. My son is also straightforward. My son took one look at the comedian and said, "Oh that guy died like eight years ago, Dad." Wow, I guess he is not so fat and happy after all. He was gluttonous, and he died. When you are gluttonous, you are excessively greedy, which means you are putting yourself first in everything you do. We need to always put God first in everything we do.

When you put your faith in the Lord, you need to look ahead, look into, and look out for. When you look ahead, you are focusing on the future. When you have sinned, learn from it and do not commit that sin again. If you are committing the same sin over and over, you are only fooling yourself.

> Now if we died with Christ, we believe that we
> will also live with him. (Romans 6:8 NKJV)

I believe that if we spiritually died with Christ and are born
again with Him in a new spiritual life, we have turned away from
sin. If you commit the same sin over and over, you are not living
a life with Jesus in it. There is no gray area with this one. God
sees everything. If you are sinning repetitively, you are a fool,
you are being fooled by Satan, and you most certainly are not
fooling our Almighty God who sees through everything. I hope
you get the point.

We must look into ways that please our God. By reading the
Word, we stay close to Jesus and away from Satan's temptation.
When our faith is strong, we look into ways to bless others. I
believe that you can show no greater love than to lead someone
to the Lord. Look into ways that you can give of yourself without
expecting anything in return.

> Take heed that you do not do your charitable
> deeds before men, to be seen by them. Otherwise,
> you have no reward from your Father in heaven.
> Therefore, when you do a charitable deed, do not
> sound a trumpet before you as the hypocrites do
> in the synagogues and in the streets, that they may
> have glory from men. Assuredly, I say to you, they
> have their reward. But when you do a charitable
> deed, do not let your left hand know what your
> right hand is doing, that your charitable deed may
> be in secret; and your Father who sees in secret
> will Himself reward you openly. (Mathew 6:1–4
> NKJV)

When we look ahead, we are focusing on a better life, a life
with the Almighty God. When your cup runneth over with the

Lord's Word, there is no room for one sip of Satan. Be in a place where you know that when you take your last breath here on earth, your eternal life awaits you. Look ahead to an eternity in heaven, being reunited with your lost loved ones of years gone by. To those of you who are hurting, look ahead to a spiritual life with no pain and suffering.

> The Lord is my rock and my fortress and my deliverer;
> My God, my strength, in whom I will trust;
> My shield and the horn of my salvation, my stronghold. (Psalm 18:2 NKJV)

I really enjoy putting more and more Bible verses into this book. I would enjoy it even more if you would put this book down, look up to the Lord, and say, "Lord, I want a new life with You in it. I confess that I have sinned. I know that my sins have separated me from you. But now, right now, I turn away from my sins, so I can live an eternity with You."

Welcome to the kingdom of God. I encourage you to pick up not my book but *the* book (the Bible). Show your humility in front of our God. Get on your knees and pray to the almighty one who is our creator. Now that you have made your commitment to Christ, I encourage you to read on in the Bible, to find a church with a pastor who teaches the Word, and to look ahead. Do not look back. Do not ever look back.

If you still have this book in your hands, I would like to share a short story with you that takes place on the golf course. I play in a golf club that has more nonbelievers than believers. I enjoy the game of golf, but I don't enjoy the mindset of some of the golfers in our group. I guess I could have taken the easier path and surrounded myself with a lot of believers on the course. But no, I took the difficult path. I guess my belief was that you keep your friends close and your enemies closer. But I do not consider the nonbelievers that I golf with enemies. I consider them future believers who could change quickly given the right motivation. Well, I am ashamed to say that I have not led anyone in this group to the Lord. Am I a failure? I do not believe so. The Bible verse that applies to my effort is this:

> A sower went out to sow his seed. And as he sowed, some fell by the wayside; and it was trampled down, and the birds of the air devoured it. Some fell on rock; and as soon as it sprang up, it withered away because it lacked moisture. And some fell among thorns, and the thorns sprang up with it and choked it. But others fell on good ground, sprang up, and yielded a crop a hundredfold. (Luke 8:5–8 NKJV)

I had a change of thought today on my approach with them. Normally when we are playing golf, I try to keep to myself and lead by example. When I fall short is when I get pulled into their arguments. I should not argue with them. I am going to, from now on, listen more. Like I mentioned earlier, God gave us two ears and one mouth for a reason. My approach with them will be like that of a doctor. I believe that many nonbelievers are in pain because of something that happened in their life, causing them to turn away from God. I am going to, from this moment on, listen to them and try to determine where their pain is. I will try to focus on the pain and not the suffering from the pain, hence the argumentative attitudes. My goal is to spread love, joy, and understanding and not try to win arguments with them. Why argue? I know what I believe. I am comfortable with my faith, and nothing that they say is going to change that. Why have a miserable life when you can have the Holy Spirit living inside of you? You are either living with the Lord in your soul or you are dead. I choose life! Sorry about that. I got ahead of myself, and we are into the next topic, listen.

To listen (my definition) is *to hear, be attentive to sound*. When you are listening, you are taking in information—in other words, acquiring knowledge. Listening is a receptor for taking in data, if you will, to send to the brain to be processed. Do you remember the old saying "You can't learn anything if you don't listen"? Now I was just telling you about my golf buddies and arguing with them. I need to turn my attention away from arguing and focus on understanding them. You are never going to lead someone to the Lord by winning an argument with them. How foolish to think, *I have just won this argument. Now they must come to the Lord.* That is not how it works. When you find the Lord, you love the Lord with all your heart, mind, and soul (remember that from earlier in the book). When you receive the Lord, you are open and receptive. When you are arguing, you have your guard up. I need to change my approach.

I need to come alongside my golf buddies and listen to them. I did not say agree with them. I will be receptive and get to understand why they believe what they believe. If I do not have answers for them, I will just tell them, "I now understand why you believe what you believe, and rather than giving the incorrect response, give me time to get you the right answer." When I can discuss the Bible with someone, I find it better working with them one-on-one. It allows for a better listening environment. There are a lot of other advantages, but the main one is I can better help them with their pain.

There was one golfer in our group who I just did not get along with from the start. We had our differences. One day, when I had a one-on-one with him, I opened up to him about my wife passing away. When it was my turn to listen, he proceeded to open up about when he lost his son in a plane crash. We had an incredibly good conversation, and I listened to him. By listening, I learned about his pain. I believe that it is this pain that kept him from having a relationship with Jesus. Now this was not the only skeleton in his closet, but it was a start. Well, I never got to finish with him. He had cancer, and we got notice that he was dying. I tried to reach out to him, but I was unsuccessful. I left him a message that I would like to go to his house and pray for him. I never heard back. The next day, he was gone. I never had the opportunity to get with him to see if he would like to receive Jesus. I need to now listen to myself and change my approach with my golf buddies. I have learned a lesson.

To learn (my definition) is *to gain knowledge.* I believe that there is a process in learning. You look, you listen, and you learn. A couple of years ago, I lost another golf buddy to amyotrophic lateral sclerosis (ALS). We were over at his house one day to share some pizza and soda. There were about five or six of us golfers there in his dining room. We laughed and told golf stories. Unfortunately, I was the only Christian in the room. We could not discuss God. I was the last one to leave, and while I was walking out the door, he grabbed me and said, "Don, I wish I would have been more religious in my life." Rather than trying to learn more about what he was thinking at that moment, I said to him, "It's not about being religious; it's about having a relationship with Jesus Christ." I wish we could have sat down and talked. The next time I saw him, he was in hospice. I was by his bedside praying for him. At that moment, my wife reached over to him and grabbed his hand. I wish I could paint a better picture of this moment. He was unconscious and motionless. When my wife touched him, she said "I would like to pray for you." At that moment, I watched his head turn ever so slightly toward her. As she was praying for him so that he could accept Jesus before his last breath, I saw him faintly taking in every word as she spoke. I was witnessing my wife leading someone to the Lord. It was one of the most beautiful memories that I have in my life. And I believe that when my wife was entering heaven later, he was holding the door open for her. I learned so much from my wife in that moment. I was looking and listening intently. That is why she was my teacher.

> That if you confess with your mouth the Lord Jesus and believe in your heart that God has raised Him from the dead, you will be saved. For with the heart one believes unto righteousness, and with the mouth confession is made unto salvation. (Romans 10:9–10 NKJV)

> Jesus said, "I am the way, and the truth, and the life. No one comes to the Father except through Me." (John 14:6 NKJV)

Now to wrap up this chapter on humility, I need to paint this picture for you. I am six three; my wife was five foot nothing standing on a book. I was successful in business; my wife supported everything I did and raised our children. I had a college education; my wife had a high school diploma. I built our house and our office from the ground up; my wife built a relationship with the Lord for our family and friends. I repeat, my wife is my teacher.

Today is March 11, 2021. It has been one year since my wife went to be with the Lord.

Fight Fear with Faith

You have come a long way. You are now on track to finding your faith. But what happens if you hit a bump in the road? What do you do when life hands you that major setback? Life is full of ups and downs. Do you honestly believe that you can make it through life without anything bad happening to you? Are you prepared for the worst when it happens? If you do your homework and plan your day ahead of time, things will go a lot smoother for you. Do you have a plan in place to reduce your stress?

Pray
Reduce
Anxiety
Yield

How do you fight fear with faith? You pray about it. Praying is your way of directly talking to God. Focus on the Lord and on His Word to reduce anxiety. And yield by putting God first. Let me give you a better explanation.

To pray (my definition) is to *make a spiritual request.* But who do you pray to? It is my belief that the fastest way to get somewhere is to follow a direct path. Some religions have you praying to idols, statues, and other objects. But what is so hard about praying directly to God? Set a schedule for regular prayer, maybe morning and night. A good time to pray would be right before a fear-filled event. I know some baseball pitchers who would be in constant prayer on the mound during a game. If you are on the mound, you have the choice of talking to yourself or talking to God. I choose God. What an awesome thought. You are with our awesome God on the mound, facing only a batter. You have a great advantage on your side. With God on your side, your fears disappear. You are fighting your fears with faith.

In 2002, I was playing baseball in an over-forty-year-old men's league. I had pitched all year as just a ninth-inning closer. I would show up at the game, get comfortable, tell some stories, and when the eighth inning would come around, I would get off the bench and start to warm up. Then when the ninth inning came up, it was my job to finish the game. Easy enough, right? Well, at the end of the season, we played at the over-forty World Series in Phoenix, Arizona. There I was enjoying my drive up to Phoenix, thinking that I would pitch in the second game for maybe one or two innings and then drive back home. I was wrong. I got a call while on the highway that our team just lost the first game of a double-elimination tournament, and the coach was asking me to start the second game. I could not believe how the fear started to kick in. My mind was racing. I had not started a baseball game in years. When I arrived at the field, I was greeted by our coach. "Hi, Don, you're going to start, and you're going to throw to a catcher you've never pitched to before." Now my anxiety was at its peak. After I threw ten pitches in the dirt, warming up in the bullpen, the catcher came up to me and said, "Have you ever pitched before"? I said, "Doesn't look like it, does it." I was so full of fear, knowing that I had to win or we were out of the tournament. I walked out onto the mound, threw some warmup pitches, took a few deep breaths, and said a prayer to God:

"Lord, bless this day. Lord, I know this is only a game, but I do not want to let my team down. But more importantly, Lord, I do not want to let You down. No matter what the outcome is today, I know that You are my God, and You will look after me. Lord, I pray in Your name. Amen."

My faith was strong, and my fears disappeared. I pitched a complete nine-inning game, and we won. After the last pitch, I gave thanks to the Lord—not for the win but because He eliminated all my fears.

Now that is only a game. What about the fears we have in everyday life? I am expecting a grandson today and am thinking of the fear those kids must be experiencing right now, knowing they have never had a baby before. This is their first one. Everyone around us is praying for them right now. They are surrounded by so much faith. The way she is handling her fears is amazing. She seems so peaceful. Now my son, that is another story. He is a nervous wreck. You get fearful when you do not know what is going to happen. But that is when you put your faith in God and give all your worries to Him. God does not worry; He knows all.

> Fear not, for I am with you:
> Be not dismayed, for I am with you.
> I will strengthen you,
> Yes, I will help you,
> I will uphold you with my righteous right hand.
> (Isaiah 41–10 NKJV)

> I sought the Lord, and He heard me,
> And delivered me from all my fears.
> They looked to Him and were radiant,
> And their faces were not ashamed. (Psalm 34:4–5 NKJV)

I want to remind you of one thing. When you pray, do not pray a memorized saying or something you have said over and over. Our God is so special, and He deserves the best you have to offer. Kneel, bow your head, clear your mind, open your heart, and let the Holy Spirit within you deliver your message. If it is a prayer that has been prayed before, it is coming from someone else and not from you. But if it is a prayer that is coming from the Holy Spirit within you, you are glorifying our God. Now that we have that clear and you fully understand what God expects from you concerning how you pray, let us move on. If not, and you still have questions, put down this book and seek more information by looking in your Bible, talking to your pastor, or confiding in a Christian friend who truly has your best interests in mind. But first, pray with me, and if you desire, add your own prayer at the end. You get the idea.

"Lord, You are so awesome, and it is my desire to get to know You. Lord, there is so much to learn about You, and I am just starting out. I know that if I follow God's plan for salvation, I will live an eternal life with You. Lord, that is my desire. You are the lamp unto my feet, and my path in life now leads to You. Amen."

Reducing anxiety (my definition) *is implementing techniques to counter stress or not knowing.* I just got off the phone with my son, and he gave me the update on the baby being born. The contractions are eight minutes apart. So, when he told me this, the first words out of my mouth were: "Son, can I pray for the both of you and your son?" He said, "Absolutely," as he put the phone on speaker. The best way to reduce anxiety is to put all your worries and fears in God's hands. If you do not know, why not hand it off to our God, who knows all. Imagine the two of them with contractions eight minutes apart. This is their first baby. They only know what they know. For what you do not know, you must put it in God's hands. Their first child, and they are putting it all in God's hands. No better time to know Jesus than when you are bringing another life into this world.

To reduce anxiety, focus on JESUS:

Just pray
Exercise
Sleep
Understand your symptoms
Stop worrying

Paul wrote in the Bible:

> For I am persuaded that neither death nor life, nor angels nor principalities nor powers, nor things present nor things to come, nor height nor depth, nor any other created thing, shall be able to separate us from the love of God which is in Christ Jesus our Lord. (Romans 8:38–39 NKJV)

> Be anxious for nothing, but in everything by prayer and supplication with thanksgiving, let your requests be made known to God. (Philippians 4:6 NKJV)

Think for a minute how much Paul loved the Lord. Philippi was where Paul established his first church in Europe. Despite being jailed, Paul wrote the book of Philippians. The main thought behind Philippians is that Jesus Christ is within you and the resurrection of Jesus Christ. That is why I live my life for the Lord, knowing He died on the cross and rose from the tomb. All this for us. Now that we are on this thought, let us talk about yielding.

Yield (my definition). It is not by coincidence that this word is placed here, and it has two meanings. Let this sink in. *First, yield means to give way to. Secondly, yield means what is produced.* There could not be a more powerful definition at this point in this book. Let me put this together for you. If you yield your life to the Lord, you will yield blessings in abundance. If I yield to the Lord and have faith in Him, He will handle all my fears. Let us pray about it:

"Lord, I am fearful, and I only know what I know. But, Lord, You are an awesome God, and You know everything. Lord, I give my life to You, and I have faith that You will protect me from all that I am fearful of. Lord, You conquer all fears. Lord, I invite You into my life to protect me from what I am fearful of. In Your name, I pray. Amen"

I will have to pick up when I get back. My phone shut off for some reason, and my daughter's two friends drove over here to tell me the contractions are five minutes apart, and I am hopping in the car to drive over to the hospital. Just got back home. No baby yet. Wait! The phone is ringing. Jameson Preston Davis—8.69 pounds! I am now a proud grandfather of a beautiful grandson. I could write a separate book on the birth of a child. I believe that the Holy Spirit within me is telling me to write on with this topic now. I am going to roll with *yield* and see what God places on my heart. But first I want to share an extremely confidential moment that I had with my son during the birth of his son. I apologize to my son now for sharing this, but I believe there is an important message in this for you. Right before my grandson was born, I sent this message to my son: "Awesome, you're getting real close son. Remember, God gave you two ears and one mouth. Listen to her needs, comfort her, and keep positive! Right now, it is all about Christina and your son. Get ready for the greatest moment of your life. It's ok to cry."

After the birth, my son called me, crying. "Dad, that was the greatest moment of my life." The reason I shared that with you is that I believe the birth of a child is a miracle and should be treated as one. Do you believe the birth of a child is a miracle? And if so, how are you going to react when you witness a miracle? Will you cry? Will you drop down to your knees and give thanks? Will you take it for granted? The choice is yours.

Close your eyes, and what do you think of when you read the word *yield*? Yes, that red triangular sign on the road that tells you to let someone else go ahead of you. And when you are proud parents of a new baby boy, what is going to happen from now on? You have a new member of the family whose needs come before yours. I do not believe that this word just showed up in my brain. It was placed here for a reason. We need to put God first in everything we do. We need to yield to Him. What an awesome thought: if every time we tried to put ourselves first, a big yield sign would be placed right in front of our face. Then we would be reminded to put God first.

At first, we might need reminders like WWJD (what would Jesus do). But the truth is when you put Jesus first, you are studying the Bible. You are going to church on a regular basis. You are getting involved in Bible studies. You are doing all these things in life because you want to fill your life with Jesus. And when you do this, it leaves no voids for Satan to root into.

When you give your life to the Lord, you reap all the blessings. Now that is not the reason you become a Christian, to get monetarily wealthy. Jesus will bless you in the way He chooses. Since I met my wife, I always tried to be the best at what I did by working hard. I always prayed to God for wisdom and discernment. I basically prayed for what I wanted but worked for what I needed. Yield yourself to the Almighty God and pray for what you have no control over. Our fear comes from not knowing the outcome or what is going to happen. I must share a story with you.

I was talking on the phone yesterday with a good friend of mine I nicknamed "Joey Saddleshoes." When I met Joe, I was walking into a business meeting with him, and he was this well-known businessman in the community who I was fearful of talking to. My boss reminded me, "Careful what you say to him."

As I said a small prayer, I looked down and thought, *This guy is wearing saddle shoes.* I am not going to be intimidated by someone wearing saddle shoes, and I was not. I found a way to fight my fears. Now multiply that over and over, and that is what it is like to have God on your side. Now that is not it. I have become good friends with Joe over the years, and he is an inspiration in my life. As we were talking and laughing on the phone yesterday, I brought up a saying that my father in-law used to tell my son all the time. He said, "God is not going to give you any more than you can handle." I told Joe I never found that in the Bible. He said, "Hold on one second." Within a few seconds, he said, "Here it is":

> So, if you think you are standing firm, be careful that you do not fall! No temptation has overtaken you except what is common to mankind. And god is faithful; he will not let you be tempted beyond what you can bear. But when you are tempted, he will also provide a way out so that you can endure it. (Corinthians 10:12–14 NKJV)

So, by yielding to a well-read, devout Christian, I stand corrected. The blessings are harvested when we put our pride aside and yield to those who know the Word. The knowledge you possess when you immerse yourself in the Word of God. It is time to pray, and add to it if you so desire.

"Lord, it is such a blessing to study Your Word and to get to know You. Lord, I give thanks and praise to You for bringing my grandson into this world. Lord, I ask that You speak to the heart of his parents and that they raise him to know You. Lord, give me wisdom and discernment in finishing the rest of this book. Lord, I fear only You, but I know that You love me and You want me to get to know You better. Lord, it is my desire to know You. In Jesus's name, we pray. Amen."

Before we move onto the next chapter, I want to point out

to you what you probably have already noticed: I have been inserting Bible verses and prayers. As you have been getting further into the book, the frequency of both the Bible verses and prayers have increased. I have been trying to prepare you for a walk with Jesus Christ. As we go through life, daily activities get more complicated. When you start your career, get married, have children, and so on, life gets harder. Decisions get more difficult to make, and you find yourself in a place where you keep saying, "I don't know." Well, you can know. You can have the answers. You can eliminate all your fears. This is done by turning your life over to Jesus Christ. Let His Word lead you. Find your wisdom by learning the Bible—not just reading it but studying it. Go to church and get to know fellow believers in Christ. Get to know your pastor. Fill your life with what is good and filter out all the bad. Start your walk with Jesus Christ in your life today. Find your faith!

Undying Devotion

UNDYING devotion (my definition) is *to have your faith last forever.* It does us no good to say, "I used to go to church." That is like saying, "I used to exercise and eat right." Does that do you any good? Do not kid yourself. I get it. Life is like a roller coaster. Every day, you have your ups and downs. When you really find yourself in trouble is when that roller coaster starts going backward. When you start falling back in life (backsliding), you take the chance of falling off the tracks.

Humans are sinful by nature, and we get that, but when we knowingly sin or sin repetitively, we are putting God to a foolish test. That is why we live for today and tomorrow, and we cast away yesterday. We have built a strong foundation. We are headed in the right direction. We have increased our knowledge to keep us on track. So, with all this effort, how can your train jump the track? Because you do not maintain yourself. You do not keep yourself fed on the Word of God. You do not worship regularly. You have no commitment. You must understand that it is a lifelong commitment, an undying devotion that gets you eternal life. Let us study this closely because we must know that we do not take the easy route. We do not follow the popular crowd. And we do not quit. We need to pray right now.

When you pray, you may want to start your day in prayer. You will pray a certain way, so you ask God to bless the day ahead of you. At the end of the day, you want to pray in a way such that you give thanks for the blessings you received today. And if anything is weighing heavy on your heart, pray for that also so you can rest with no worries, now that you have handed that off to God. Let us pray a morning prayer, and at the end of this chapter, we will give thanks for the day.

"Lord, I thank You for this day. Lord, as I face this day, I ask You for wisdom to make good decisions. Lord, I pray that the decisions I make will honor You in everything I say and everything I do. Lord, I ask You for strength to carry out and to defend these decisions that are made in Your honor. Lord, it is my desire to get to know You more and more each day. Lord, I pray for my family, that they too can get to know You more each day. Lord, I ask You to forgive me for my sins, and with Your guidance, it is my desire to turn away from my sin and have eternal life with You, Lord. I pray in Your name. Amen."

Pray for what you are to encounter today. Pray that Jesus will take all your worries away. And pray that He will watch over you. And remember to pray from the heart. You are praying directly to the Lord, one-on-one. Do not use someone else's prayer. It will honor God if someone else prays for you, but do not recite a prayer written by someone else. It is okay to use other prayers as templates if you are starting out on your walk. But remember to pray from the heart.

As you read the final two chapters of this book, I would like to again add to the presentation that you have been given. I started off with a foundational format: the ABCs; how to investigate; the truth; humility; facing fears. Along the way, I slowly incorporated Bible verses and prayer. I have tried to gradually show you a way of how you are going to walk with the Lord for the rest of your life with undying devotion. I have showed you how to prioritize your life by laying out your foundation with the five Fs. Your faith (God) comes first in everything you do. Not only does God come first, but it is now what you are all about. Let me give you an example by borrowing an old saying: working at a job is what you do, but being a Christian is now who you are. You need to understand the difference. Having a job pays your bills, but being a Christian tells you how to live your life. And when I say life, I do not just mean today and tomorrow. I am referring to the rest of your life, undying devotion.

> Grace be with all those who love our Lord Jesus
> Christ in sincerity. Amen. (Ephesians 6:24 NKJV)

Paul wrote Ephesians while in prison in Ephesus. Ephesus was an ancient city whose ruins are in what is now Turkey. Like many cities at that time, it was an important Greek trading city that survived many battles and traded hands numerous times.

To remain loyal to this concept, you need to pray about your options in life and make the right decisions that honor God. The wrong decisions can knock you off the path of righteousness. That is why I frequently say to those I love, "May God bless the path that you take and the choices that you make." I am praying that God will be the lamp unto your feet and keep you on track in life.

If you noticed, I just gave you a Bible verse, the author, and a brief description of where it was written. When you study the Bible and you read the verses, you need to know who is writing them and where it was written so you can understand why it was written and in the proper context—all so you get the proper interpretation. To me, interpretation is critical to understanding the Bible. If a nonbeliever reads the Bible, they are most likely going to have just a surface-level meaning of what the Bible says. But when you study the Bible, you get a complete and full understanding of what the Bible is telling you. Nonbelievers seem to take most of what they know out of context, just to support their argumentative narrative. There is quite a difference in perception when you study something versus just reading it. I missed an opportunity to put this Bible verse in because I was driving home a point. Let us look at "lamp to my feet."

> **Y**our word is a lamp to my feet.
> **A**nd a light to my path.
> (**P**salm 119:105 NKJV)

The Word of God is the lamp to my feet, and the path is the way to eternal life. God has a way of delivering a message to me. I just noticed that when I typed out this Bible verse, the first letter in every line spells Y-A-P. The slang meaning of Yap is mouth. I believe God is wanting me to hold the tongue and give you more Bible verses.

> Who is the man who desires life,
> And loves many days, that he may see good?
> Keep your tongue from evil,
> And your lips from speaking deceit. (Psalm 34:12–
> 13 NKJV)

This Bible verse hits home with me because, with my Parkinson's brain operating at half capacity, I would have trouble lying. I find it hard enough just to recall the truth. If I were lying to you, you would know it right away. And I believe that I need to keep my tongue from evil and my lips from telling lies so I can see many good days. I remind you at this time what the purpose of this book is and why I wrote it with this prayer:

"Lord, Your Word is Thee Word, in our life and nothing compares to it. This is just a simple book with its sole purpose to lead nonbelievers to the Bible. Lord, more importantly, I believe that the Bible was written so we could study and learn about You. Lord, we want to know You, and when we do, we want to lead others to You. An eternal life with You, Lord, is my main desire. In Jesus's name, I pray. Amen."

There is one point in my prayer that I would like to elaborate on. I was reminded of it by my brother who is studying divinity at the university level. It is our belief that we worship God. The Bible was written by man to learn more about and bring us closer to God. We worship no book. We worship God. We live in a world where millions of people have not heard of or have turned away from the Gospel. When you have turned your life to the Lord, you do not hide His message like a secret. When you know the Lord, you want to share the message with those who do not know it. It is my prayer that if this book can be helpful in just leading one lost soul to the Lord, it will be worth all the sleepless nights when the Lord was using me to write this book. I humbly say *write* because I believe I am just being used as a messenger to help deliver His message to those who want to have a relationship with Jesus Christ.

I started this chapter off like a new day with a prayer. I would like to end this day with a special prayer too.

"Lord, I thank You for this day. I got to see my grandson face-to-face for the first time today. Lord, it will be my honor in helping his parents to teach him Your Word. Lord, I believe his birth is a miracle. I listened to some of the pain his mom went through in delivery and the confusion that my son dealt with in trying to comfort her. Lord, I believe that with all the pain and all the confusion, it was worth every moment to receive your gift of this miracle I call my grandson. And when I looked into his eyes for the first time and he looked into mine, I knew they brought one more life into this world that wants to know You, Lord. I give You thanks and praise. In Your name and on this special day, I pray. Amen."

I have told you how to start your day and how to end your

day. What you do in between those times is your choice. I pray that you choose wisely.

> At that time, the disciples came to Jesus saying, "Who then is greatest in the kingdom of heaven?" Then Jesus called a little child to Him, set him in the midst of them, and said "Assuredly, I say to you, unless you are converted and become as little children, you will by no means enter the kingdom of heaven. Whoever humbles himself as this little child is the greatest in the kingdom of heaven. Whoever receives one little child like this in my name receives Me." (Mathew 18:1–5 NKJV)

Jesus is saying we need to give up our so-called status here on earth and humble ourselves like little children. If we cannot do this, we cannot enter heaven.

> Then Jesus said to His disciples, "Assuredly, I say to you that it is hard for a rich man to enter the kingdom of heaven. And again, I say to you, it is easier for a camel to go through the eye of the needle than for someone who is rich to enter the kingdom of God." (Mathew 19:23–24 NKJV)

What is more important to you, your wealth here on earth or eternal life in the kingdom of heaven? That needs to be an instantaneous answer. If you must think about it, you are in trouble. Let us pray again.

"Lord, it is my desire to live an eternal life with You in heaven. Lord, I need to understand and accept the concept that whatever wealth we earn and store up here on earth has no bearing on us entering your kingdom. Lord, I know that our salvation is a gift from You. You died on the cross so that our sins could be forgiven, and by turning away from our sins and accepting You, we will be given eternal life. In Jesus's name, we pray. Amen."

Why am I praying more with you now? Because that is what you do when you turn your life to the Lord. When faced with decisions, you pray about it. When you want your children to be safe, you pray for them. You pray about those things in life you have no knowledge of or control over. Seek His wisdom, guidance, and help every chance you get.

It was my intention when I wrote this book that I would keep it under one hundred pages. It was written as a guide to lead you to the Bible, which in turn will bring you closer to the Lord, which ultimately will culminate in eternal life in the kingdom of heaven. That is what I want. Isn't that what you want? Is it not worth you giving him your undying devotion? Let us move on to the final chapter. But first, put down this book and say a prayer on your own. It should be a prayer that worships God. Ask him to look over you. And always pray in His name. See you again in the next chapter.

Legacy of Love

IF you are still reading this book, it could only mean one of two things. Either I am a phenomenal writer, or I haven't convinced you to find your faith. I have this final chapter to convince you to pick up the Bible. But remember, you have free will to believe or not. Please be open-minded, and I will give it my best effort. I can give you my reasons why you should turn your life around and live a life filled with faith. But I have been reminded to tell you that I cannot be the reason you turn your life to Christ. I am just a lowly messenger delivering His message. Salvation is a gift from God, and it will only be by God's grace that He will give us this gift. We are born sinful in nature, and we need to repent. If you need a better explanation of this, ask your pastor. He can tell you. Let us continue with the legacy of love.

Leave a legacy of love—this is one of my most powerful arguments. When you leave this world, how do you want to have those you love remember you? If you follow the Bible with its helpful hints, you will realize in an instant what adds to your legacy and what puts reminders of you in the minds of those you love. Do you leave someone a lot of money or a lot of stuff, or do you leave a memory to those you love that during your lifetime you gave of yourself to the point where you could no longer give anymore? My father in-law recently passed away, and the legacy he left in my mind is the latter. He would not give you a dollar out of his pocket, but he would break his back to help you. That was the way he was raised, and that was the legacy he passed on to me and my children and their children, and so on ... When he passed, the only thing that went to me was this legacy, and I feel like I received the greatest gift of all from him. I love him more for that. He was six inches shorter than me, but I always looked up to him. I would rather be like someone I admire rather than look like someone who no one admires. Ponder on that.

When you leave a legacy of love, you touch people's hearts. To touch someone's heart, you need to give of yourself. Here is a letter from my daughter's best friends who came into town for the anniversary of my wife's passing. This letter is hanging above my desk:

> Patty lives on every day in the warmth of Natalie's smile, the joy of Jimmy's laughter and in your never-ending love for your children, family, and friends. We cannot thank you and Patty enough for the great gift you gave us in Natalie. The love Natalie shows us comes directly from the love she was shown growing up. We cannot begin to imagine or even understand how hard this year has been. Patty was truly a beautiful woman- beautiful in body, mind, and soul. We are so lucky to have been loved by her and to continue to share in the Davis family love.
> We love you, Liz, Ana, and Bri.

When you leave a legacy of love, you get those you love writing letters like this. You have touched people to the point that they would drive and fly in from out of town to hand-deliver a letter with flowers to the father of one of their friends. I cannot begin to express to you how much that meant to me. But I guess I am showing how much it meant by putting it in this book.

How finding your faith benefits you: When you find your faith, you establish a format for how you are going to live your life. And if you are a head of a household, a leader in the community, or have an influential position at work or any position where you encounter others, you can influence them to live a life of faith by delivering God's message. As I have said before, there are abundant blessings for those who help others turn their life around to find their faith. It is easy to fall off a cliff, but it takes a lot of work to climb a mountain. Sometimes you need help to reach the peak or to keep from falling all the way down. Finding your faith instills a presence in you that you are focused on God, and you will not be undone. With faith, you love what you do, how you do it, and who you bless with your faith-filled efforts.

There is a lot to say about love. I covered the topic of love in a previous chapter, but it can always bear reviewing again. There is not enough love in this world to go around, but there is plenty of hate to wrap around the world many times. Remember, in the absence of love, there is hate. If you walk in faith, you spread love and joy in everything you do. When you know you have faith, you recognize the difference between happiness and joy. You want to live a life where you are consistently filled with joy rather than a life where you are happy-sad-happy-sad-happy-sad. Life has enough up and downs. You need to be emotionally stable and consistent in your inner self so you do not fall out of life's daily roller coaster when it is heading out of control. It is the desire of many to be in control of their destiny and able to see happenings before they occur. To stay on track, you must stay focused. When you stay focused, you will notice things that occur, and you can act on them before they become a roadblock in front of your path.

Biblical principles. When you live your life by instituting biblical principles, you live your life the way God wants you to. When you insert God's plan into your life, you set your compass heading in the right direction. God will only bless you when you are living your life with Him in it. There are no gray areas there. You either follow His plan or you do not. I want to remind you of John 3:16 again.

> For God so loved the world that he gave his one
> and only Son, that whoever believes in him shall
> not perish but have eternal life.

I have one question for you right now, and it is straightforward, and you already know the answer. After hanging on and reading this entire book, you know the answer. If you do not know the answer, let me pray for you. And that question you need to ask yourself right now is: Heaven or hell? Where do you want to spend eternity?

Did I scare you with that question? Well, I am not sorry for asking it. If you do not believe in God, you believe in Satan. It is either one or the other. There is no middle ground with this question. Do you know where you are going to go when you take your last breath here on earth? And do you fully realize that you do not know when you are going to take your last breath? At this time, I would like you to pray about your decision. Put on some soft Christian music, close your eyes, and pray. When you come back, I would like to share one more poem that I penned just for you:

> In absence of light, there is darkness.
> In darkness, there is no life.
> To journey, we need light.

Life is a journey, not a destination.
The world believes a lot can happen to you when
you don't plan.
I believe that eternal life is what happens when
you follow God's plan.

If you have the correct answer, welcome to the kingdom of God! If you have the wrong answer, hand this book to someone else. I worked too hard on it to let it burn in your fire. For those of you who want to live a life with Jesus, you need to turn back to chapter 2 and read about the ABCs. You need to place yourself with an attentive pastor. You need a Bible to study the Word of God. And you need to attend the church where your pastor teaches.

It may sound funny, but just like my newly born grandson, we are born into this world in diapers, and some of us are even wearing diapers when we leave this world. But when we enter heaven, we are pain-free. We have no physical deformities that can get in the way of us worshipping our creator. If you are heading to the hotspot down south, how about telling your so-called scientists to come up with something better than the big bang bust. I am tired of laughing at that theory.

Then many false prophets will rise up and deceive
many. And because lawlessness will abound, the
love of many will grow cold. But he who endures
to the end shall be saved. And this gospel of the
kingdom will be preached in all the world as a
witness to all the nations, and then the end will
come. (Matthew 24:11–16 NKJV)

This Bible verse addresses those who are false prophets. Those who are in it for their glory and not to give all the glory to God will suffer the consequences. I will be clear that any effort on my part toward this book is strictly for leading new believers and lost souls to the Lord. I am just a messenger. Now I will make my exit. It is my hope that when this book is read or is no longer needed, it gets passed to someone who could benefit from it. The benefit I got from writing this book was it brought me closer to God. The knowledge I gained from talking to devout Christians in my family and close friends who were critical of my writing to make sure I did not cross the line was priceless. These are family members and friends who came alongside me with Christian advice so I could make it through the toughest moment of my life, when Patty was called to heaven.

I take comfort in knowing that the Lord was leading me on this mission. He was there by my side for all the sleepless nights. He was there through all my personal trials and tribulations. And I hope He is there for my family and friends who will edit and make corrective recommendations on the content of this book. I already told them I can handle any constructive criticism they throw my way. This book is not and never will be about me. As I have said throughout the whole book, and I will say it again, the purpose of this book is to lead nonbelievers and lost souls to the Lord.

Another note I would like to make at this time. I just came back from the dentist so he could work on my two cracked teeth that happened last night. You cannot imagine the pain I have been going through to finish this book for you. But I know that my pain pales in comparison to the pain that was endured by Jesus when He was crucified on the cross so our sins could be forgiven. As my pain level increases, I leave you with this poem that God blessed me with:

> We only know what we know of what we have
> been taught.
> We know nothing about nothing of what we
> know not.

Those who have died for us, they will not be
forgotten.
Those who have died for themselves, their
memory will be rotten.
When we give of ourselves, we have given our all.
When we give for ourselves, we are going to fall.
When we have found God's direction to know
where we are,
He will love us and comfort us and will not let
us stray far.
And the sins of the world can cut like a knife,
But when you study the Bible, you have been
born a new life.

May God bless the path that you take and the
choices that you make.

Epilogue

I HAVE suffered many hardships in life. I have gone under the surgical knife more than twelve times, with more than 150 stitches and counting. Although this may sound significant to many, it pales in comparison to what happened to me in 2020. No matter what history may tell us about the great pandemic of 2020, I was given a different perspective to remember. March 11, 2020, was the day I lost my wife, Patty, to cancer. She fought a five-year battle with ovarian cancer. Patty endured five surgeries, twenty-eight chemotherapy treatments, and even a ten-day period where I was her nurse, giving her IVs every eight hours to treat peritonitis caused by a rupture in her small intestines. Now it may not sound like much for someone to administer IVs, but I left one important detail out.

Back in 2013, I developed Parkinson's disease. Parkinson's is a neurodegenerative disorder that affects dopamine-producing areas of the brain. Let me get back to my wife. Can you imagine me shaking with Parkinson's while hooking up an IV to my wife's port, which was installed in her chest less than six inches away from her heart? Add to that, stressful situations magnify the effects of the tremors or shaking of the Parkinson's. I wish I would have taken video of that to show others just exactly what we were going through.

My wife, Patty, was a devout Christian for most of her life. She had studied the Bible cover to cover for many years. She devoted her life to teaching a women's nondenominational Bible study every Thursday morning for many years. So, you guessed it. Everything Patty and I did together had to revolve around her Thursday-morning ministry. There never was a scheduling conflict. I, on the other hand, was raised in a household that rarely read the Bible. We went to church for weddings, funerals, and special occasions. Growing up, I never would have imagined going to church on a Sunday just to go to church. So, my knowledge of the Bible was extremely limited.

You may wonder what brought me to the Lord. One night, when I first met Patty, I was pitching in a men's city league baseball game. At that time, I was in my late twenties, and I still enjoyed playing the game. I pitched in college for only one year, so I never really got my fill of playing baseball. So, there I was one night, ready to deliver my newly developed split-finger fastball to the plate. Well, that fastball never touched the catcher's mitt. All I can remember from that moment was getting struck by a line drive off the side of my head. I was knocked out cold. When I came to, I was lying on the ground, and I could see players huddled over me. I could see, but I could not speak. I was trapped inside my body. When I felt the side of my head and there was a golf ball–sized welt on my right temple, I went into shock. It was the strangest feeling I have ever experienced.

I can remember a paramedic squeezing my hand and telling his partner that they had to rush me to the hospital immediately. They could not wait for the ambulance. At that moment, I was humbled like I have never been humbled before. I realized my life could end that quickly. And I was powerless to do anything about it. When I recovered from that traumatic experience, I came to the realization that I needed a change in my life. From that moment on, I was going to have a new life, with Jesus Christ as my Lord and personal Savior.

My direction in life changed dramatically. I was going to do well, but it was only going to happen with Jesus in my life. My wife was my teacher, and I would learn to pray about everything. If I was going to do something at work that was new or different, her response was always, "Did you pray about it?" My wife wanted us to work in the church together as a family, the two of us and our two children. We ended up working at the church's coffee shop on Sundays for many years. It was our coffee shop ministry. I worked six days a week at my job, and on the seventh day, I made coffee for people going to and coming out of church. After everyone left, we cleaned and sanitized the entire coffee shop from top to bottom. I enjoyed doing this because I felt that we had a great pastor, and we were helping his staff get the Word out to the community. I always humbled myself when it came to talking about the Lord because there were so many believers who were better read than I was, and I did not want to take away from the message that the pastor at the church was delivering.

When I first read the Bible, I read it cover to cover. I would go to the gym and ride the stationary bicycle for an hour every night. This would give me time to read a few chapters out of the Old Testament and a few chapters out of the New Testament while riding the bike. What I noticed about reading the Bible was everyone would see me reading it in the gym, and they would have their opinion of the Bible. It is amazing how much negativity you can hear from people about the Bible when, in fact, they have never actually read the Bible or studied it. At the start, reading the Bible was quite simple. The word *Bible* means book. And when someone says "Amen," they are saying, "The truth." So, when a passage is read in church and you answer, "Amen," you are agreeing that the truth is being spoken. So, if you take this approach, you can see how simple it can get. Study what you read, and it will come to you. I have always believed that if you seek the truth, you will need to find the first written word on the subject before it has had a chance to be rewritten.

In 2007, I took my wife on a trip to visit a traveling exhibit of the Dead Sea scrolls in San Diego. That is your first written word. That discovery was made in the 1940s when they found the site of Qumran. Qumran is where the scribes had written and stored the scrolls. I will never forget watching my wife as she carefully examined all the documents and artifacts in the exhibit. I was, at that time, starting to realize just how strong my wife's faith was and how important it was to her.

So, what has led me to write this book on faith? I observed my wife during her last weeks of her life. Her faith in Jesus Christ meant everything to her. Not once did she cry out, "Why me?" or did she beg for other options to delay the inevitable. The whole time I was with her, she was excited because she was going to go with Jesus. I remember walking her around the house when she would keep waking up every fifteen minutes at two or three in the morning. She had a look on her face that I will never forget. She was going up to heaven to be with our creator, and it was just a matter of a few days. She was so excited. I was amazed how strong her faith was. She was a true believer. I realized at that time that I too wanted to have a faith that was that strong—a faith that would get me through all the trials and tribulations in life. Isn't that what you want? Find your faith in Jesus Christ.

Printed in the United States
by Baker & Taylor Publisher Services